3

Workbook
Grammar Connection

STRUCTURE

THROUGH

CONTENT

SERIES EDITORS

Marianne Celce-Murcia

M. E. Sokolik

Hilary Grant

HEINLE
CENGAGE Learning

Australia • Brazil • Japan • Korea • Mexico • Singapore • Spain • United Kingdom • United States

HEINLE
CENGAGE Learning

Grammar connection 3: Structure through content workbook
Marianne Celce-Murcia, M. E. Sokolik, and Hilary Grant

Editorial Director: Joe Dougherty

Publisher: Sherrise Roehr

Consulting Editor: James W. Brown

VP, Director of Content Development:
  Anita Raducanu

Acquisitions Editor, Adult & Academic ESL:
  Tom Jefferies

Director of Product Marketing: Amy Mabley

Executive Marketing Manager: Jim McDonough

Senior Field Marketing Manager:
  Donna Lee Kennedy

Product Marketing Manager: Katie Kelley

Cover Image: ©Robert Harding World Imagery/
  Getty

Editorial Assistant: Katherine Reilly

Senior Production Editor:
  Maryellen Eschmann-Killeen

Print Buyer: Betsy Donaghey

Production Project Manager: Chrystie Hopkins

Production Services: Parkwood Composition
  Services

Cover Designer: Linda Beaupre

ISBN-13: 978-1-4130-0844-9

ISBN-10: 1-4130-0844-5

Heinle
20 Channel Center Street
Boston, MA 02210
USA

Cengage Learning is a leading provider of customized learning solutions with office locations around the globe, including Singapore, the United Kingdom, Australia, Mexico, Brazil, and Japan. Locate your local office at **www.cengage.com/global**

Cengage Learning products are represented in Canada by Nelson Education, Ltd.

Visit Heinle online at **elt.heinle.com**

Visit our corporate website at **www.cengage.com**

Printed in the United States of America
3 4 5 6 7   19 18 17 16 15

Contents

Simple Present Tense: Statements/Questions/ Short Answers; Adverbs of Frequency

PART ONE	Simple Present Tense: Statements/Questions/Short Answers

A Complete the sentences with the best verb from the box.

watch	register	waste	make	communicate	work
review	have	participate	be	use	

1. Gerardo: How's your new instructor?

   Ariana: She's very good. She _____*doesn't waste*_____ time in class. (not)

2. Nicole: Where's your planner?

   Coby: I _____ a daily planner. (not)

3. Marleen: _____ your teacher _____ the syllabus in class once in a while?

   Michael: No, he _____. (not)

4. Juan: _____ your parents _____ TV at night?

   Matthew: Yes, they _____.

5. Juliana: You always get such good grades.

   Cristina: I _____ with a great study buddy.

6. Solin: _____ new students _____ early for classes?

   Alana: No, only old students do.

7. Raul: The instructor really likes Sam.

   Carolina: He always _____ in class.

8. Debbie: I never get promotions at work.

   Juliana: Do you _____ with your boss?

9. Jaime: Does the university _____ a tutoring center?

   Pablo: No, it _____.

10. Isabella: Henry always gets a good grade on his essays.

    Violet: That's because he _____ revisions on written work.

11. Alberto: Jenny _____ a really successful student.

    Rula: Yes. She studies a lot.

B Write questions with the words in parentheses. Then write a short answer.

1. (Linda / waste time / on the Internet / at night)

    _____ *Does Linda waste time on the Internet at night?* _____

    Yes, _____.

2. (new students / register for classes today)

    _____?

    No, _____.

3. (they / discuss / irregular verbs / in class today)

    _____?

    No, _____.

4. (the students / communicate / with the teacher/ by Internet)

    _____?

    Yes, _____.

5. (your children / watch / a lot of TV)

    _____?

    No, _____.

6. (you / be /a happy person)

    _____?

    Yes, _____.

7. (Claudia / use / the library / often)

    _____?

    No, _____.

8. (good student / participate / in class)

    _____?

    Yes, _____.

9. (your friends / be / successful students)

    _____?

    Yes, _____.

10. (you / review / your notes / before a test)

    _____?

    Yes, _____.

C **Circle the correct answer to complete the sentence.**

1. Gerardo _____ in the library every evening.
   a. studys   b. study   (c.)studies   d. does study

2. Kimmie _____ like to visit the Tutoring Center.
   a. doesn't   b. don't   c. not   d. isn't

3. Juan _____ good grades in English.
   a. get   b. is   c. isn't   d. gets

4. Liza and Karina _____ in class tonight.
   a. are'nt   b. not be   c. aren't   d. don't

5. My friends _____ to the Student Union after class every night.
   a. goes   b. doesn't go   c. isn't go   d. go

6. _____ you walk to campus?
   a. Are   b. Do   c. Aren't   d. Doesn't

7. I _____ notes for students who are absent.
   a. take   b. taken   c. not take   d. am

8. Does Britney get good grades? _____
   a. Yes, she do.   b. Yes, she is.   c. Yes, she's.   d. Yes, she does.

9. The classroom _____ computers.
   a. have   b. haves   c. has   d. doesn't haves.

10. My instructor never _____ time in class.
    a. waste   b. doesn't waste   c. don't waste   d. wastes

PART TWO   **Adverbs of Frequency**

A **Write a sentence using the words in parentheses and an adverb of frequency.**

1. (Maria / get to class on time) (100%)
   _____ Maria always gets to class on time. _____

2. (Tom / be punctual) (5%)
   _____

3. (we / talk) (20%)
   _____

4. (Lucia and Roberto / go to the tutoring center) (0%)
   _____

5. (I / participate in debates) (80%)
   _____

6. (my sister / work at home) (40%)

_____

7. (my mother / use the Internet) (5%)

_____

8. (my family / go out to eat on Fridays) (90%)

_____

9. (I / read the newspaper) (50%)

_____

10. (they / study in the library) (80%)

_____

B **Answer the questions. Use adverbs of frequency in your answers.**

1. What do you do on Mondays? _____

2. What do you do every day? _____

3. What do you do every summer? _____

4. What do you do in the morning? _____

5. What do you do once a month? _____

C **Unscramble the questions. Then answer them with an adverb of frequency.**

1. exam / ever / do / notes / review / your / before / an

_____ *Do you ever review your notes before an exam?* _____

_____ *No, I never review my notes before an exam.* _____

2. do / you / Internet / how / use / the / often

_____

_____

3. food / you / do / ever / waste

_____

_____

4. you / TV / how / watch / often / do

_____

_____

5. on / work / how / often / you / do / weekends

_____

_____

6. for / ever / do / register / you / things / online

_____

_____

7. you / extracurricular / do / participate / in / activities

_____

_____

8. in / country / your / often / how / communicate / do / you / family / home / your / with

_____

_____

9. a lot / use / cell phone / you / do / your

_____

_____

10. doctor / the / visit / you / often / do

_____

_____

11. class / perfect / ever / do / you / achieve / attendance / in

_____

_____

Putting It Together

GRAMMAR

A **Rewrite the sentences with mistakes. If there are no mistakes, write "C."**

1. He go to work every day.   _He goes to work every day._

2. She does not participate in class often.   _____

3. He does communicate with his parents?   _____

4. I not a very successful student.   _____

5. We are review the answers at the
   end of class.   _____

6. Do successful student use a daily
   planner?   _____

7. Yes, I'm.   _____

8. She watchs four hours of TV a day. _____

9. How often you visit the tutoring center? _____

10. Always I go to class on time. _____

11. She always drinks coffee on the morning. _____

12. When do you study? _____

B **Complete the conversation. Use the words in parentheses.**

Andrea: Hi, Bruno. How's your wife doing in school?

Bruno: Not so great. She __*doesn't have*__ good grades. (not have)

Andrea: _____ to the tutoring center? (go)

Bruno: Yes. She _____ the center twice a week, at least! (visit)

Andrea: That's good. _____ a study buddy? (have)

Bruno: No, _____.

Andrea: _____ in class? (participate)

Bruno: No. _____ shy. _____ a lot. (be) (not talk)

Andrea: _____ her homework? (do)

Bruno: Sometimes she _____ to do her work. (forget)

Andrea: _____ a daily planner? (use)

Bruno: No, _____.

Andrea: _____ notes in class? (take)

Bruno: Well, she hardly ever _____ notes. The instructors _____ too fast. (take) (talk)

Andrea: _____ with her instructors? (communicate)

Bruno: I don't think so.

Andrea: You know what? I'll be her study buddy!

Bruno: Thanks, Andrea!

Complete the clues and solve the puzzle.

Across

3. I sit at the front of the room and _____ a lot.

6. The instructor prepares a _____ every year.

Down

1. The teacher gives an _____ at the end of each semester.

2. I take _____ during class.

4. I read the _____ every night.

5. I use a _____ to organize my schedule.

PART ONE	Review of *Wh-* Questions: *What, Who, When, Where, Why, How*

A Complete the questions with a question word.

1. _____*What*_____ does the teacher do on Fridays?

2. _____ does your Spanish class start?

3. _____ do I need to register early?

4. _____ is the first day of registration?

5. _____ is the parking lot?

6. _____ is your mother?

7. _____ happens on the first day of class?

8. _____ works in the library with you?

9. _____ building is the cafeteria in?

10. _____ bus stops in front of the school?

11. _____ one is easier to learn, French or English?

B Circle the letter of the correct question.

1. It's fine.
   a. How are you?   b. How old are you?   ⓒ How's your class?

2. At 10:15.
   a. What time does class begin?   b. What class do you have?   c. Where is your class?

3. They're in my bag.
   a. Are these your books?   b. Where are your books?   c. Which ones are your books?

4. My friend does.
   a. Who is your friend?
   b. Who drives you to class?
   c. Who do you call every day?

5. It's at 8:00 PM.
   a. When is the party over?
   b. What time is it?
   c. When is the party?

6. It means "begin."
   a. What commences tonight?
   b. What does "commence" mean?
   c. What is "commence?"

7. We have debates.
   a. What happens in class on Mondays?
   b. What do we debate?
   c. What is a debate?

8. Mr. Banderas does.
   a. Who is Mr. Banderas?
   b. Who teaches your class?
   c. What does Mr. Banderas do?

9. The tall one.
   a. Which woman is Maya?
   b. Where is Maya?
   c. What does Maya do?

10. The Spanish class.
    a. Which class is your favorite?
    b. When is Spanish class?
    c. What do you study?

11. Because it's very interesting.
    a. Is it interesting?
    b. What is history?
    c. Why do you like history?

C Complete the questions with *what* or *which*.

1. _____What_____ country are you from?

2. _____ town are you from, New Haven or Hamden?

3. _____ subject do you like the most?

4. We offer Russian and Chinese. _____ language do you want to study?

5. _____ classes do you have this semester?

6. You can register on Monday or Tuesday. _____ day do you want to register?

A **Complete the sentences with tag questions.**

1. You're a pretty successful student, _____ *aren't you?* _____

2. You don't have any more classes today, _____

3. He's an English instructor, _____

4. My friends don't call very often, _____

5. We're late, _____

6. Alana always registers for classes late, _____

7. Mr. Wright, the counselor, talks a lot, _____

8. Twenty units of English is a new requirement, _____

9. They don't offer a lot of classes, _____

10. You're not angry, _____

11. The course catalogue is complicated, _____

12. You don't sleep a lot, _____

13. Ms. Breton's class isn't very interesting, _____

14. Fedor has a daughter, _____

B **What do you say? Read the situations. Then write sentences with tag questions.**

1. You want to confirm that an acquaintance lives in New York now.

   _____ *"You live in New York now, don't you?"* _____

2. You think your sister weighs 120 lbs.

   " _____ "

3. You think your friend isn't six feet tall.

   " _____ "

4. You think your friend doesn't speak Portuguese.

   " _____ "

5. You're at a concert that hasn't started. You think you and your friends are early.

   " _____ "

6. You think your brother isn't sad.

   " _____ "

7. You think you're too loud.

   "_____"

8. You're at a party. You think your friend wants to leave.

   "_____"

9. You're at a restaurant. You think your friend doesn't like fish.

   "_____"

10. You think the museum opens at 10:00 AM.

    "_____"

11. You see a dog. You don't think that dog is friendly.

    "_____"

12. You see a group of children walking. You think they walk to school every day.

    "_____"

Putting It Together

GRAMMAR

A **Rewrite the questions with mistakes. If there are no mistakes, write "C."**

1. He doesn't like to study, doesn't he.   *He doesn't like to study, does he?*

2. When he has class?   _____

3. Bob doesn't have a counselor, does Bob?   _____

4. Who is your English instructor?   _____

5. You're new, are you?   _____

6. What happens after class on Fridays?   _____

7. She doesn't have a lot of experience, has she?   _____

8. They don't talk a lot, do they?   _____

9. Why I need five classes this semester?   _____

10. What subject you like?   _____

11. We don't have homework, don't we.   _____

12. What time does class?   _____

B Complete the conversation with question words.

Hugo: Hey, Felipe. _____How_____ are your classes?

Felipe: Great! I really like my classes this semester.

Hugo: _____ classes do you have?

Felipe: Psychology and English.

Hugo: _____ one is your favorite?

Felipe: Psychology.

Hugo: _____ is your instructor?

Felipe: Dr. Brown.

Hugo: _____ do you take psychology? That's not your major.

Felipe: It's a requirement for all students.

Hugo: I start school soon.

Felipe: _____ do you begin?

Hugo: Next semester. I register today.

Felipe: _____ 's your major?

Hugo: Business administration.

Felipe: That's cool. _____ classes do you take next semester?

Hugo: English and Business Administration I.

Felipe: _____ are the classes: in the morning or in the evening?

Hugo: I think they're both in the evening. At least I hope so.

Felipe: Well, good luck!

Hugo: OK. See you around next semester.

Find the words in the puzzle and circle them.

```
A  P  W  F  P  M  G  Z  U  M  B  Y  F  O  D
P  Y  L  B  D  V  U  O  O  J  R  D  X  T  H
P  E  X  J  X  T  H  H  L  E  F  P  N  C  K
O  M  C  J  E  S  H  L  Q  A  E  H  E  E  A
I  R  O  L  E  S  N  U  O  C  T  S  B  J  Z
N  Y  E  J  Y  K  I  I  N  Z  R  A  T  B  M
T  R  T  W  R  R  N  C  K  U  Z  L  C  U  G
M  I  Z  C  E  N  C  J  O  A  P  M  R  S  G
E  S  X  M  G  I  Q  C  E  N  K  B  G  O  V
N  I  E  E  W  T  F  R  H  E  E  L  J  A  Q
T  N  E  U  R  H  T  D  X  M  W  F  W  F  K
T  I  C  S  S  E  L  E  C  T  W  U  I  J  J
B  M  N  M  N  A  I  W  E  T  C  Z  T  M  W
Z  V  D  M  W  Q  Z  O  S  Q  F  H  Q  X  P
V  J  F  O  J  M  S  N  K  Z  T  G  C  Q  X
```

APPOINTMENT

CATALOG

COUNSELOR

COURSE

REQUIREMENT

SELECT

SUBJECT

Linking Verbs;
Imperative Verbs

PART ONE   **Linking Verbs**

A **Complete the sentences with a linking verb. Some verbs may be used more than once. (Answers will vary.)**

stay	become	be	seem	get	sounds
appear	remain	feel	smell	taste	

1. I _____feel_____ sick. My stomach hurts.

2. We _____ home on Sundays. We go out on Saturdays.

3. You _____ tired. You're so quiet.

4. Your house _____ clean.

5. During family vacations, the dogs _____ at the house with a dog sitter.

6. The dog _____ friendly. He wags his tail a lot.

7. Sandra _____ very sick. She _____ in the hospital.

8. You _____ beautiful. That dress is perfect for you.

9. What a wonderful dinner party. The food _____ so good.

10. I _____ impatient when my children don't listen.

11. Claire has a sore throat. She _____ terrible when she talks.

12. I always _____ hungry at 12:30.

B **Write a question with linking verbs using the words in parentheses. Then write an answer that is true for you.**

1. (feel sleepy / after eating a big meal) _Do you feel sleepy after eating a big meal?_

_____

2. (have / body aches right now) _____

   _____

3. (coffee / taste good to you) _____

   _____

4. (how / feel right now) _____

   _____

5. (usually stay home / on the weekends) _____

   _____

PART TWO — Imperative Verbs

A Match column A with column B.

A	B
a. Don't go to bed _____ 6 _____	1. in class more.
b. Wear _____	2. something.
c. Join _____	3. your textbook.
d. Take _____	4. a gym.
e. Don't eat _____	5. a lot of carbohydrates.
f. Call _____	6. too late.
g. Drink _____	7. your time.
h. Open _____	8. a coat.
i. Review _____	9. the window.
j. Participate _____	10. the doctor.

B Give advice. Use sentences from exercise A.

1. I have to get up early. _____ *Don't go to bed too late.*

2. I want to lose weight. _____

3. I'm so late! _____

4. I'm really thirsty. _____

5. It's hot. _____

6. I have a big test. _____

7. I always get bad grades. _____

8. I feel really sick. _____

9. I want to get in shape. _____

10. It's cold outside. _____

GRAMMAR

A Rewrite the sentences with mistakes. If there are no mistakes, write "C."

1. He am very busy today.   _____ *He is very busy today.*

2. Don't forget to shut the door!   _____

3. The food look and smells great. _____

4. Juan looks like happy.   _____

5. I'm growing a stomachache.   _____

6. You wash your hands please.   _____

7. Anna stays at school late when
   she has tutoring.   _____

8. His dad seem tired.   _____

9. Help me bring in the groceries. _____

10. You feel sick, stay in bed.   _____

11. She is in the house.   _____

12. If Mark takes the medicine, he
    doesn't gets sick.   _____

B What do people do in your country for these situations? Use imperatives.

1. If you have a headache, _____ *lie down somewhere that is quiet and dark.* _____

2. If you have a stomachache, _____

3. If you want to lose weight, _____

4. If you have a sore throat, _____

5. If you have a cough, _____

6. If you want to find a job, _____

7. If you want to buy a car, _____

8. If you want to save money, _____

■ VOCABULARY

Find the words in the puzzle and circle them.

```
S  B  F  I  S  I  R  N  I  L  K  P  Z  L  I
S  A  K  H  A  J  K  R  T  X  A  W  W  L  A
L  Z  O  C  C  F  Y  U  C  T  K  M  L  T  N
L  T  M  X  F  E  E  B  H  I  V  N  R  W  Q
I  J  C  J  Z  P  M  V  Y  E  E  Z  K  O  U
H  D  J  E  H  S  A  R  E  S  R  I  C  J  N
C  O  E  H  T  X  P  E  S  R  Z  O  S  A  Q
R  N  Q  O  K  L  J  M  W  Y  Q  T  S  X  F
S  S  Z  B  Q  C  A  R  X  K  G  Q  C  Q  A
D  O  R  C  T  I  U  U  U  H  W  W  W  M  K
Y  G  R  E  L  L  A  I  N  J  U  R  Y  D  R
O  B  Y  D  M  H  F  T  U  K  K  B  M  P  U
A  P  X  Q  H  W  G  K  X  S  T  U  H  L  A
U  D  Y  G  P  K  D  U  W  D  R  F  F  U  G
E  S  J  E  J  F  Z  P  U  C  Y  W  R  W  V
```

ALLERGY

BURN

CHILLS

FEVER

FLU

ILLNESS

INJURY

ITCHY

NORMAL

RASH

SHOT

SNEEZE

SORE

Ability: *Can/Could/Be Able To;*
Reflexive and Reciprocal Pronouns

PART ONE   Ability: *Can/Could/Be Able To*

A **Complete the sentences with affirmative or negative *can, could,* or *be able to.*
(Answers will vary.)**

All children are so different. When Desmond was ten months old, he
___was able to walk___ (walk) by himself. Patrick _____ (walk) at ten
months, but he _____ (stand up) by himself. Julia is 12 months
old now and _____ (walk) yet, but she _____ (talk)! My
sister's daughter, Zoe, is seven months old. She's _____ (sit up). She
_____ (crawl), though. My oldest daughter, Sophie, _____
(dress herself) until she was six! But her cousins are only two and they're (put
on) their own shoes.

B **Write a question with *can.* Then write a response that is true for you.**

1. play an instrument _____ *Can you play an instrument?* _____

   _____ *No, I can't. OR Yes, I can.* _____

2. sing _____

   _____

3. drive _____

   _____

4. build a Web site _____

   _____

5. cook _____

   _____

6. play soccer _____

   _____

7. run a mile _____

_____

8. throw a ball _____

_____

C Complete the sentences with *be able to.*

1. Last year I broke my leg. I _*wasn't able to walk.*_ (walk)

2. Kerry has a sore throat. She _____ (sing)

3. My father got new glasses. He _____ now. (drive)

4. I hurt my hand. I _____ (go rock-climbing)

5. Ginny is only 11 months old. She _____ yet. (talk)

6. Last week I was sick. I _____ with you. (go out)

PART TWO   **Reflexive and Reciprocal Pronouns**

A Complete the sentences with a reflexive pronoun.

1. Emily is only two, but she already dresses _*herself*_.

2. Carina and Finn introduced _____ at the party.

3. Nick hurt _____ while mowing the lawn.

4. The Grants enjoyed _____ at the movies last weekend.

5. Ms. Daisy is 98 years old. She has difficulty taking care of _____.

6. I taught _____ piano at the age of five.

7. We congratulated _____ after we finished the project.

8. The children usually behave _____ in my class.

B Complete the sentences with *by* + a reflexive pronoun.

1. Emily is only two, but she already gets dressed _*by herself*_.

2. Carina and Finn played _____ in the house.

3. I finished the project _____.

4. The cat came home _____.

5. You have to study for the test _____.

6. We painted the house _____.

7. Samuel stands _____ now.

8. You and your sister have to go to the party _____.

C Complete this conversation between two mothers, Jane and Sara, with the correct form of a reflexive verb from the box and with a reflexive pronoun.

dress	behave	enjoy	bathe	feed	control

Jane: How is Jeremy doing?

Sara: Great. He __*feeds himself*__ now. How's Stevie?

Jane: She's great. She _____ now. She puts on sweaters and everything. And now she _____, too. She loves the bath.

Sara: Wow! That's great. How's Peter?

Jane: He's very smart, but he doesn't _____ in school. He's very naughty.

Sara: Oh? What does the teacher say?

Jane: She says he has to _____ more.

Sara: But does he _____ in school. Does he have fun?

Jane: Sometimes. But not when he's in trouble.

D Read another conversation between Jane and Sara. Complete the conversation with *by* + the reflexive pronoun or a reciprocal pronoun.

Sara: It's nice that Jeremy and Stevie like to play with __*each other.*__

Sara: I also like that they play by themselves!

Jane: Yes, now we can enjoy _____.

Sara: Jeremy does a lot _____ now.

Jane: You're lucky. That gives you time _____.

Sara: Yes, but most of the time I spend cleaning the house.

Jane: Do you clean it _____?

Sara: No. My husband cleans, too. We help _____.

Jane: That's nice.

Sara: Hey, I saw your husband at the school conference.

Jane: I was sick so he went _____.

Sara: He's very nice.

Jane: Yes, he is.

Putting It Together

■ GRAMMAR

A **Rewrite the sentences with mistakes. If there are no mistakes, write "C."**

1. He walks to school by hisself.   *He walks to school by himself.*

2. Do they play well with each other?   _____

3. We helped one another in college   _____

4. Yesterday I can't talk.   _____

5. My leg is broken. I'm not able walk.   _____

6. We introduced each other at
   the meeting.   _____

7. My son couldn't walk until he
   was 15 months old.   _____

8. She hurt her when she went
   rock climbing.   _____

9. She cans play the piano.   _____

10. We were able to see the Pope.   _____

11. He goes to the bathroom by herself.   _____

12. Clara taught herself to speak English. _____

B **Write about two things you or someone you know *can* do now that couldn't be done ten years ago.**

   I can speak Spanish now. Ten years ago I couldn't speak Spanish.

1. _____

2. _____

C **Write about two things you or someone you know *can't* do now that could be done ten years ago.**

   I can't run ten miles now. Ten years ago I could run ten miles.

1. _____

2. _____

Find the words in the puzzle and circle them.

```
D  F  L  S  N  L  E  B  P  Z  M  U  L  G  J
S  R  K  H  B  O  Z  N  C  J  B  N  V  D  H
E  J  E  T  G  Q  I  Q  D  U  I  B  X  Q  H
O  Z  Z  S  D  Y  R  T  M  F  H  D  J  K  S
H  J  N  T  S  K  E  D  A  S  E  O  S  G  P
S  F  F  L  J  H  P  A  N  V  R  J  H  B  V
N  D  E  A  T  N  E  M  N  O  R  I  V  N  E
O  U  F  L  B  P  A  R  E  N  L  E  Y  A  U
T  G  P  A  E  J  T  A  S  Q  S  P  S  W  V
U  F  B  S  O  K  W  Y  I  E  M  R  D  B  T
P  C  E  D  Z  V  O  A  J  E  L  A  M  F  O
C  A  M  S  N  C  R  J  S  U  U  F  B  Q  K
F  M  Q  S  T  R  D  W  Z  F  R  D  R  U  B
R  Y  R  S  F  I  S  S  I  J  W  H  A  C  J
S  J  T  W  K  D  W  I  W  I  R  W  M  D  S
```

DRESS HERSELF

ENVIRONMENT

OBSERVATION

PUT ON SHOES

REPEAT WORDS

Present Progressive: Statements/Questions/Short Answers; Simple Present vs. Present Progressive

PART ONE | Present Progressive: Statements/Questions/Short Answers

A Use the words to create sentences in the present progressive.

1. I / work / late / every night / this month

   I am working late every night this month.

2. my tutor / not / help / me / a lot / in math / this year

   _____

3. you / be / very quiet / in class / this semester

   _____

4. my sister / fill out / an application / for a loan / online

   _____

5. we / apply / for a grant / to fix the house

   _____

6. my grandparents / not / receive / much income / at all / these days

   _____

7. my husband and I / not / communicate / well / lately

   _____

8. I / participate / in class / a lot

   _____

B Write the question using the words given. Then give an answer that is true for you.

1. do / your / homework _____ *Are you doing your homework?*
   _____ *Yes, I am. OR No, I'm not.* _____

2. use / the computer _____
   _____

3. take / a lot of classes this semester _____
   _____

4. earn / any income / now _____
   _____

5. do / work study _____
   _____

6. you / instant messaging / with anyone / right now _____
   _____

C Write an information question using the words given. Then give an answer that is true for you.

1. where / you / live? _____ *Where are you living?* _____
   _____ *I am living in an apartment.* _____

2. where / you / take classes? _____
   _____

3. where / they / hire / students / on campus? _____
   _____

4. what / you / eat / for lunch? _____
   _____

5. what / your best friend / do / now? _____
   _____

6. what / you / take / this semester? _____
   _____

D Observe the students and teacher in your class now. What are they doing?

1. _____

2. _____

3. _____

4. _____

5. _____

6. _____

7. _____

8. _____

| PART TWO | Simple Present vs. Present Progressive |

A Complete the sentences with the simple present or present progressive form of the verb.

1. (participate) Julia usually ____*participates*____ in class, but she ____*isn't participating*____ now.

2. (register) I _____ for class this week. They only _____ students on Mondays and Fridays.

3. (communicate) Sometimes couples from different cultures (not) _____ well. Andrea and Hugo (not) _____ well at all lately.

4. (review) The instructor _____ the subjunctive this week. She usually _____ grammar on Fridays.

5. (happen) What _____ in class these days? What usually _____ at the end of the semester?

6. (live) My parents _____ on Maple Avenue, but they _____ with me now while their condo gets painted.

7. (have) The local boutique rarely _____ sales, but this week it _____ a big sale.

8. (hit) My daughter _____ her brother a lot, but this week she (not) _____ him at all.

9. (introduce) At these functions, he typically _____ everyone. But this week he's not here, so everyone _____ themselves.

10. (dress) Two year olds usually (not) _____ themselves, but my daughter _____ herself just like a big girl.

B **Complete the sentences with the correct form of the verbs in parentheses.**

1. (remember) I _____*remember*_____ her! She was my kindergarten teacher.

2. (play) They _____ my favorite song!

3. (not understand) I _____ you. Could you speak slower?

4. (believe) My parents _____ in God.

5. (love) We _____ your new house!

6. (think) I _____ about you all the time.

7. (eat) Slow down! You _____ too fast.

8. (get) My sister _____ a grant to pay for college.

9. (like) I _____ my night classes.

10. (go) My friends and I _____ to work by car.

C **Write a question for the answer given.**

1. _____ *Are they hiring students to work in the library?* _____

   Yes, they're hiring students to work in the library.

2. _____

   Ms. Bradley is a lawyer.

3. _____

   I usually play golf on the weekends.

4. _____

   Amy is in Canada studying French.

5. _____

   No, I'm not working this week.

6. _____

   I'm living with my parents until I can find a new apartment.

7. _____

   Sometimes we go to the movies on Friday nights.

8. _____

He's speaking Swahili.

9. _____

I am taking two English courses next semester.

10. _____

Gerardo's going to a soccer game.

11. _____

Yes, I know Maria Cecilia

12. _____

No, I don't understand French.

Putting It Together

GRAMMAR

A Circle the letter of the correct answer to complete the sentence.

1. My cousin always _____ people's names.

   (a.) forgets   b. is forgetting   c. Forget

2. I _____ for financial aid.

   a. am apply   b. applying   c. 'm applying

3. The team _____ for pizza after every game.

   a. go out   b. going out   c. goes out

4. What are you doing? _____

   a. I'm a lawyer   b. I'm being happy.   c. I'm finishing my homework.

5. We _____ about the new financial aid program for international students.

   a. are not knowing   b. don't know   c. are know

6. He _____ really well lately.

   a. is singing   b. 's sing   c. sings.

7. They _____ at a hotel now.

   a. 're staying   b. stay   c. don't staying

8. Miguel _____ you.

   a. isn't hear   b. doesn't hear   c. don't hear

9. I _____ a therapist once a week.

   a. seeing   b. saw   c. see

■ VOCABULARY

Find the words in the puzzle and circle them.

```
R  M  A  H  X  V  V  E  E  X  E  E  T  E  B
L  H  Z  I  S  S  X  X  S  R  T  N  K  M  A
S  S  J  Q  D  Q  X  L  U  N  A  F  J  O  Q
S  O  K  F  L  Q  P  V  V  R  E  D  C  C  W
R  U  X  I  J  G  S  C  G  C  E  P  K  N  R
M  J  Q  N  D  W  P  G  R  A  H  J  X  I  Z
K  R  T  A  I  C  R  S  D  Z  A  Q  F  E  W
N  R  C  N  P  K  A  L  E  G  D  W  E  M  R
T  N  I  C  A  L  I  P  V  Q  Q  G  E  P  L
B  N  O  I  N  N  O  I  T  I  U  T  G  Z  B
P  K  Q  A  E  E  J  B  B  F  Q  L  T  R  S
Z  X  F  L  O  A  N  L  X  B  B  Z  G  N  O
E  Z  O  Y  B  Q  B  L  P  T  N  U  U  C  D
K  U  Q  C  R  N  F  M  R  K  A  V  S  L  S
M  U  K  O  Y  M  I  Y  M  A  K  Y  C  P  V
```

AID

DEADLINE

EXPENSE

FEE

FINANCIAL

GRANT

INCOME

LOAN

TUITION

Phrasal Verbs: Transitive/Separable;
Phrasal Verbs: Transitive/Inseparable;
Phrasal Verbs: Intransitive/Inseparable

PART ONE · Phrasal Verbs: Transitive/Separable

A Complete the sentences with the correct form of a phrasal verb from the box. Use each phrasal verb only once.

think through	start out	figure out	do over	turn in
hand out	give back	look over	point out	put off

1. I'm ____figuring out____ how much money I need for college.

2. Cristina's mother is _____ cupcakes to the children.

3. Sebastian always _____ doing his homework till later.

4. The magazine (not) _____ manuscripts sent in by authors.

5. My son is _____ his project. The teacher said it wasn't acceptable.

6. We _____ our assignments in the morning.

7. The family is _____ the difficult decision to stay or move.

8. I _____ my work before I hand it in.

9. My children _____ every morning with a good breakfast.

10. She _____ the students' mistakes.

B Identify the parts of the sentence. Underline the phrasal verb and circle the object.

1. My grandmother is now _looking up_ (information) on the Internet.

2. Always read a contract over before signing it.

3. Write your ideas down on paper.

4. I start my customers out with a nice appetizer.

5. The instructor hands our tests back the very next day.

6. Carina is thinking over the problem.

7. Figure it out yourself!

8. The bank robber turned herself in to the police.

C Rewrite the sentence. Separate the phrasal verb and use a pronoun for the object.

1. Don't put off going to the dentist. _____ *Don't put it off.* _____

2. I always read through a contract. _____

3. Write down the guests' names. _____

4. Start out your day with exercise. _____

5. My husband thinks through problems carefully. _____

6. My daughter is figuring out a math problem. _____

7. The teacher is handing out pencils for the test. _____

8. The officer pointed out the best route to take. _____

PART TWO   **Phrasal Verbs: Transitive/Inseparable**

A Complete the sentences with the correct form of a phrasal verb. Use the words in parentheses to help find a synonym from the box. Use each phrasal verb only once.

find out	end up with	think about	go over
work through	get through	come across	call on

1. I always (discover) _____ *come across* _____ words I don't know when I'm reading.

2. Selena (get) _____ information about community events and puts it on her calendar.

3. We (finish) _____ one chapter every day.

4. My mother (contemplate) _____ her children all the time.

5. Let's (read through) _____ our tests together.

6. The instructor (ask) _____ Juana more than any other student in class.

7. We don't do enough work in class so we (finish with) _____ too much homework at the end of the week.

8. First the instructor (solve) _____ any problems, then she introduces new material.

B Unscramble the words to make questions and statements.

1. to work / the homework / do / want / how / on / you ?

   How do you want to work on the homework?

2. reading / the / first / go / let's / over

   _____

3. all / the / time / think / I / you / about

   _____

4. you / getting / all / material / through / are / the ?

   _____

5. Internet / across / I / come / old / friends / all / the / time / on / the

   _____

6. class / usually / the / teacher / on / calls / volunteers / during

   _____

7. are / we / all / of / through / working / our / problems

   _____

8. more / your / end / do / than / up / classes / always / with / men / women ?

   _____

PART THREE **Phrasal Verbs: Intransitive/Inseparable**

A Complete the sentences with the correct form of a verb in the box.

get ahead	give up	get behind	think about	keep up	sign up

Luca: Hi Pedro. How are you doing?

Pedro: I'm OK. I _'m getting behind_ in my classes, though.

Luca: Why's that?

Pedro: Well, I'm taking five classes this semester and I have a part time job.
I just can't _____.

Luca: I understand. It's crazy. I _____ by studying until 3:00 in
the morning.

Pedro: Whoa. I can't do that. I'm going to _____ for tutoring at the
center. The tutor does the homework with you.

Luca: Well, good luck. Don't _____. You'll do fine.

Pedro: Thanks. You should _____ going to the tutoring center too.
        See you later!

Luca: Later, dude.

B **Give true answers to the following questions.**

1. What are you getting ahead in?

   _____ *I'm getting ahead in my math homework.* _____

2. What are you getting behind in?

   _____

3. What are you keeping up with?

   _____

4. What are you catching up on?

   _____

5. What are you signing up for?

   _____

6. What are you giving up?

   _____

Putting It Together

GRAMMAR

A **Underline the phrasal verb. If there's an object, circle it. Then rewrite the sentences if there are mistakes. If there are no mistakes, write "C."**

1. I'm working(it)on today.   *I'm working on it today.*

2. She's putting her work off till later.   _____

3. The journalist is writing down.   _____

4. He needs to do over it.   _____

5. The teacher was pointing the
   grammar mistakes out.   _____

6. My girlfriend's thinking a lot about
   her new job.
   _____

7. I can keep up with my sister
   when we run.
   _____

8. He's catching it up to me.
   _____

9. Look it up the information online.
   _____

10. We're starting out the meeting
    with a vote.
    _____

11. I'm putting off it till later.
    _____

12. My son is signing up for soccer.
    _____

B Below is a list of transitive phrasal verbs and objects. Create sentences with the
verbs and the objects. (Answers will vary.)

Phrasal verbs	Objects
hand out	the party
call on	our homework
figure out	the outline
put off	too much food
think through	the new rules
look over	updating my résumé
give back	the contract
end up with	a new computer program
think about	the history assignment
go over	a difficult problem
work on	tests
turn in	more students

1. _____ I'm working on the outline for history now. _____

2. _____

3. _____

4. _____

5. _____

6. _____

7. _____

8. _____

9. _____

10. _____

Complete the clues and solve the puzzle.

Across

4. I read one _____ of the book last night.

6. The teacher gives us an _____ every day.

Down

1. The _____ this week is Health in the Workplace.

2. The first _____ is usually full of mistakes.

3. First we prepare an _____.

5. We often have a class _____ about current events.

Simple Past: Statements/Questions/ Short Answers; Common Irregular Past Forms; Simple Past Time Expressions: Words/Phrases/Clauses

| PART ONE | Simple Past: Statements/Questions/Short Answers; Common Irregular Past Forms |

A Read the sentence in the simple present. Then write an affirmative sentence in the past using the same verb.

1. Paola usually goes to work at 8:00 AM.

   This morning _____ *she went at 9:00.* _____

2. We always buy books at the local bookstore.

   Today _____

3. I usually pay the rent on time.

   This month _____

4. The instructor usually teaches young children.

   This week she _____

5. I usually keep my car in the garage.

   This week _____

6. My husband always comes home at 6:00 PM.

   Last night _____

7. I never meet celebrities.

   Yesterday _____

8. In the morning, the children usually read books.

   This morning _____

9. Miguel and Selena usually see each other three times a week.

   The week _____

10. We often give donations to one charity only.

    This year _____

11. The instructor usually begins the class with a quiz.

    Today _____

12. I usually write invitations by hand.

    This time _____

B **Write questions in the past with the words given.**

1. you / go / the concert   _____*Did you go to the concert?*_____

2. who / the conductor   _____

3. what / instrument / he / buy   _____

4. where / the concert   _____

5. when / the audience / leave   _____

6. who / write / the music   _____

7. you / met / the musicians   _____

8. someone / play / violin   _____

9. they / composers   _____

10. who / play / the piano   _____

11. when / conductor / arrive   _____

12. where / the musicians   _____

C **Complete the conversation using the past tense.**

Mateo: _____*Did*_____ you _____*hear*_____ (hear) about the concert on
       Friday night?

Ariel: No, I _____.

       How _____ it?

Mateo: It _____ great!

Ariel: Who _____ he conductor?

Mateo: Franz Schmidt. He _____ (come) from Germany just for
       this concert.

Ariel: What _____ they _____ (perform)?

Mateo: Two Beethoven symphonies.

Ariel: _____ the tickets _____ (cost) a lot?

Mateo: Yes, they _____. I _____ (pay) a lot for them. Seventy-five dollars each.

Ariel: Wow! _____ it worth it?

Mateo: Yes, it _____. We _____ (have) a great time.

Ariel: Who _____ (go) with you?

Mateo: My cousin, Ana.

Ariel: _____ she _____ (come) from Boston to go to the concert with you?

Mateo: Yes. She _____ (get) here on Wednesday. She's a pianist, you know.

Ariel: I _____ (think) she _____ (be) a violinist.

Mateo: No, but my sister is.

Ariel: _____ she _____ (go) to the concert, too?

Mateo: No, she _____ (not / can). She _____ (have) an exam the next day.

Ariel: Next time tell me about the concert. I'd love to go.

Mateo: Ok. That would be fun!

D Write a sentence in the past that is true for you using the words given and a time expression.

1. We ate in a restaurant last night.   *We didn't eat in a restaurant tonight.*

2. I usually drink tea in the morning.   _____

3. They had a lot of food at the party.   _____

4. She talked about the volunteer program.   _____

5. He led my group in the discussion.   _____

6. She conducted the orchestra last week.   _____

A Complete the sentences with the correct time expression from the box.

after	until	in	last	from…to	before

1. I was born _____*in*_____ 1975.

2. We lived in Russia _____ 1989 _____ 1991.

3. _____ we arrived in the United States we bought a business and a house in Boston.

4. _____ we left Russia we sold everything.

5. _____ week my sister graduated from college.

6. My mother worked as a musician _____ she died.

B Write a sentence in the past that is true for you using the words given and a time expression from the box.

after	until	in	last	from…to	before

1. be / born _____

2. live / (city or town) _____

3. start / school _____

4. call / my friend _____

5. get / home _____

6. begin / study English _____

Putting It Together

GRAMMAR

A Complete the conversation with the correct form of the verb in parentheses.

Gerardo: I _____*went*_____ (go) to Rosa's school play last night.

Veronica: How _____ (be) it?

Gerardo: It _____ (not be) good.

Veronica: Why not?

Gerardo: A lot of crazy things _____ (happen).

Veronica: Like what?

Gerardo: They _____ (stop) the play in the middle because the curtain _____ (fell).

Veronica: What? _____ anyone _____ (get hurt)?

Gerardo: Yes. The lead actress.

Veronica: _____ she _____ (go) to the hospital?

Gerardo: Actually, I _____ (offer) to drive her.

Veronica: Really?

Gerardo: Yes, but after I _____ (leave) to get the car, I _____ (discover) something.

Veronica: What?

Gerardo: Someone _____ (steal) my car!

Veronica: Gosh! _____ you _____ (call) the police?

Gerardo: Yes, two police cars _____ (come). But before they _____ (can) help me, they _____ (crash) into each other.

Veronica: What a night!

Use the clues to solve the puzzle.

Across

1. they look and listen

3. Mozart played the _____.

5. performance

6. Mozart

Down

2. a person who directs an orchestra

4. the violin

7. a person who is skilled in music

Lesson ⑧

Past vs. Present:
Used To; Past State
or Habit: *Used To/Would*

PART ONE	Past vs. Present: *Used To*

A Complete the sentences with the correct form of the verb in parentheses.

1. (take, drive) Now I _____*take*_____ the bus to work, but I __*used to drive*__ our car.

2. (use) Now we _____ reusable cloth bags to put our groceries in, but we _____ the plastic bags from the store.

3. (drive) Now my brother _____ a hybrid car, but he _____ an SUV.

4. (recycle, throw) Now our neighbors _____ their garbage, but they _____ everything into the same bin.

5. (buy) Now we _____ fruits and vegetable from local farms, but we _____ them from the large supermarket.

6. (produce) Now the electrical plant _____ electricity with wind power, but it _____ it by burning coal.

7. (clean) Now my sister _____ with nontoxic cleaners, but she _____ with bleach and ammonia.

8. (keep) Now we _____ the thermostat at 58 degrees Fahrenheit in the house, but in the winter, we _____ it higher.

B Write *yes/no* and information questions with the words *given* + *used to*. Then respond with answers that are true for you.

1. (live / in Istanbul) _____ *Did you use to live in Istanbul?* _____

_____ *Yes, I did. OR No, I didn't.* _____

2. (where / live) _____

_____

3. (work / in a bank) _____

_____

4. (what / do) _____

_____

5. (where / study) _____

_____

C **Complete the conversation with the simple present, simple past tense, or *used to* + verb. (Answers will vary.)**

José: Jasmin, someone (tell) _____*told*_____ me that you (live) _____*used to live*_____ in New York.

Jasmin: Yes, I _____. I loved it.

José: (live) _____ you _____ with your family?

Jasmin: I (live) _____ with my family, then I (move) _____ into a small apartment and got a roommate.

José: Where did you live?

Jasmin: I (live) _____ in Queens, then I (move) _____ to Manhattan.

José: What was that like?

Jasmin: My neighborhood (be) _____ great. There (be) _____ a lot of nice shops and I (go) _____ to the outdoor market every morning.

José: But (be) _____ the people friendly?

Jasmin: Oh, yeah. I (know) _____ all the neighbors in my building. I (not know) _____ anyone in the condominiums where I live now.

José: (be) _____ there a lot of traffic?

Jasmin: Yes, but I (use) _____ the subway. And I (take) _____ buses. Here you have to drive everywhere.

José: Where (work) _____ you _____ ? Did you have to travel far?

Jasmin: No, not at all. I (live, work) _____ and _____ in the same neighborhood!

José: Sounds great.

Write about things you did and didn't use to do.

1. _____ *I didn't use to walk to work. Now I walk every day.* _____

2. _____

3. _____

4. _____

5. _____

6. _____

PART TWO   **Past State or Habit:** *Used To/Would*

A **Complete the sentences with** *would* **or** *wouldn't* **plus a verb from the box.**

get	go	walk	travel	spend	rescue	speak
stay	call	argue	make	bark	practice	see

1. My sister used to live on the beach. She _____ *would walk* _____ on the beach every morning.

2. I used to work at the animal help society. We _____ abused animals all the time.

3. My husband used to work in an emergency medical organization. He _____ all over the world.

4. My father used to travel for business. Sometimes we _____ him for weeks at a time.

5. I used to work in Brazil on the border with Colombia. I _____ Spanish and Portuguese all day long.

6. My brother used to play the piano very well. He _____ two to three hours a day.

7. My parents used to live with us. We _____ with them every day.

8. You used to be such a cute baby. You _____ everyone smile.

9. We used to live in Alaska. Sometimes we _____ outside for days because of the cold.

10. I used to study a lot. Sometimes I _____ the whole night doing my homework and studying for exams.

11. My family used to belong to a country club. Sometimes we _____ there for the whole weekend.

12. I used to have a German shepherd dog. He _____ if anyone came near my children.

13. My friends and I used to go out every weekend. They _____ me on Thursday and we'd make plans for Friday or Saturday.

14. We used to work in New York. We _____ home till 9:00 every night.

Putting It Together

■ GRAMMAR

A Write about things you used to do.

1. When I was a baby I _____

2. When I was in high school I _____

3. When I was in my home country I _____

4. When I lived in my last place I _____

5. A few years ago I _____

6. When I started learning English I _____

B Describe what your home life was like when you were a child. Use *would*.

1. _____ *We would eat eggs and sausage every morning.* _____

2. _____

3. _____

4. _____

5. _____

6. _____

C Rewrite the sentences with mistakes. If there are no mistakes, write "C."

1. He use to call his mother every day.   *He used to call his mother every day.*

2. I didn't used to drive on the freeway. _____

3. There used to be a lot of heavy
   traffic downtown. _____

4. We would went to church every Sunday. _____

5. They were used to do a lot of homework. _____

6. I was used to buying fruit in the
   open market. _____

7. My instructor used to live in
   the suburbs. _____

8. She would talk for hours. _____

■ VOCABULARY

Find the words in the puzzle and circle them.

```
O   O   N   A   T   R   P   Y   V   N   R   D   C   Q   E
S   K   Y   S   C   R   A   P   E   R   O   U   N   G   T
I   Q   E   B   T   F   C   I   S   O   C   U   R   G   V
M   C   N   S   G   R   G   I   H   Y   Q   R   L   A   Y
N   M   Q   P   B   H   E   R   F   M   W   B   H   A   L
T   B   B   X   B   Y   O   E   C   F   C   A   N   Z   P
K   Y   N   O   H   B   A   Y   T   T   A   N   O   X   D
T   A   R   M   H   S   P   J   E   C   J   R   C   J   A
Q   W   L   G   H   S   A   K   Z   E   A   V   T   B   U
K   E   I   O   M   D   R   S   L   C   M   R   J   R   E
C   E   P   C   Z   A   T   G   N   I   D   L   I   U   B
N   R   X   A   M   B   M   S   U   B   U   R   B   B   D
J   F   G   X   O   N   E   Z   T   J   L   K   B   X   P
O   W   V   V   I   N   N   E   K   B   E   Z   S   Y   F
D   W   C   I   F   N   T   Q   H   W   I   C   O   I   F
```

APARTMENT   SHOP

BUILDING   SKYSCRAPER

FREEWAY   STREETCAR

MARKET   SUBURB

NEIGHBOR   TRAFFIC

NEIGHBORHOOD   URBAN

RURAL

Past Progressive;
Time Clauses: *While/When*

PART ONE	Past Progressive

A There was a fire in an apartment building yesterday morning. What were all the residents doing when the fire alarm went off? Use the words in parentheses to make sentences.

1. (I / watch TV)   *I was watching TV.*

2. (Fred and Gina / have a discussion) _____

3. (the Bakers / play board games) _____

4. (Miss Daisy / take a bath) _____

5. (Selena / talk on the phone) _____

6. (Roberto / download music) _____

7. (Angelina / feed the dog) _____

8. (Margot and Megan / watch TV) _____

9. (Timmy / put on his shoes) _____

10. (the baby / feed herself) _____

11. (Liz / apply for a loan online) _____

12. (my sisters / do their homework) _____

B Write a question using the words in parentheses. Then write a sentence saying what you were really doing at the time.

1. (you / 10:00 AM / surf the Internet) *Were you surfing the Internet at 10:00 AM?*

     At 10:00 AM I wasn't surfing the Internet, I was sitting in class.

2. (Becky / yesterday / in class / participate) _____

_____

3. (your mother / this morning / at home / clean the house) _____

_____

4. (you and your friend / after lunch / talk on the phone) _____

_____

5. (your brothers / on Friday / mow the lawn) _____

_____

C **Complete the e-mail with the simple past or past progressive.**

Hi Adriana,

   Sorry I (not call) _____*didn't call*_____ you yesterday, but I (have)
_____ such a busy day. My brothers and I (help) _____
my sister move all day long. We (begin) _____ to pack at 8:00
the night before. And in the morning we (pack) _____ still
_____. From the afternoon to the evening my brothers (move)
_____ the boxes from the house to the truck. They (make)
_____ three trips with the truck! I (not load) _____
the truck at the house. I (clean) _____ the new apartment. I
(scrub, wash, vacuum) _____ floors, _____ walls, and
_____. I (be) _____ so tired. Finally, by 8:00 PM all her
stuff was at the new apartment. Then my sister (decide) _____ to
start unpacking. So we (unpack) _____ boxes until this morning. I
need to sleep now! I'll call you in a few hours.

   Love,

   Nadia

| PART TWO | Time Clauses: *While/When* |

A **Complete the sentences with the simple past or past progressive.**

1. I (work) _____*was working*_____ in my office while my husband (play)
_____*was playing*_____ with the children.

2. We (have) _____ a discussion when the phone (ring)
_____.

3. When the parade (end) _____ we (cross) _____
the street.

4. The teacher (collect) _____ the exams when the last student (stop) _____.

5. The children (laughing) _____ while the clown (perform) _____.

6. We (play) _____ golf when lightning (strike) _____.

7. While I (run) _____ I (listen) _____ to music.

8. When the package (arrive) _____, we (open) _____ it.

9. The class (make) _____ noise while the instructor (teach) _____ a lesson.

10. The students (talk) _____ when the teacher (walk) _____ in.

11. I (burn) _____ my hand while I (cook) _____.

12. While we (get) _____ ready, the power (go) _____ out.

B Write an information question with *what* in the past using the information in parentheses. Use *when* and *while.* Then write the answer.

1. (Gina / read a magazine) (Felipe / paint the house)

_____What was Gina doing while Felipe was painting the house?_____
_____She was reading a magazine._____

2. (you / eat dinner) (power / go out)

_____

_____

3. (your family / camp in Maine) (I / take my exams)

_____

_____

4. (the instructor / correct papers) (dean / walk in)

_____

_____

5. (you / exercise) (stereo / play)

_____

_____

6. (they / sleep) (a man / robbed their house)

_____

_____

7. (we / go outside) (weather / get warm)

_____

_____

8. (he / driving to the store) (he / see the accident)

_____

_____

Putting It Together

■ GRAMMAR

A Write sentences in the past with information from the chart. Use *when* and *while*. (Answers will vary.)

	Abdul	Farid
8:00	Get up	Take a shower
9:00	Have breakfast	Do homework
10:00	Watch TV	Wait for bus
11:00	Clean the kitchen	Arrive at the school
12:00	Make a sandwich	Have lunch in the cafeteria
1:00	Drive to school	In English class
2:00	Register for classes	Visit the financial aid office
3:00	Go to the bank	In language lab
4:00	Work out at the gym	Work in the bookstore

1. 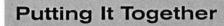 _While Abdul was getting up, Farid was taking a shower._

2. _____

3. _____

4. _____

5. _____

6. _____

7. _____

8. _____

9. _____

■ VOCABULARY

Use the clues to solve the puzzle.

Across

1. the Sahara

5. a mountain that erupts

8. the Atlantic and the Pacific

10. the Andes and the Rockies

11. There are seven of these in the world.

12. lower than a mountain

Down

2. the Nile and the Amazon

3. The earth shakes.

4. Hawaii is an _____.

6. Smoke comes out of a _____.

7. Our planet is called _____.

9. The Grand _____.

Future—*Be Going To* vs. *Will:* Forms; *Be Going To* vs. *Will:* Uses; Present Progressive and Simple Present for Future

PART ONE Future—*Be Going To* vs. *Will:* Forms

A Finish the sentences in column A with the verbs in column B.

Column A

1. I _____*d*_____ hike down the canyon with a sprained ankle.

2. _____ Debra going to be comfortable in her sleeping bag?

3. Sam _____ drive all of us.

4. _____ you going to clean out the cooler?

5. Jorge and Linda _____ put up the tent after they eat.

6. _____ I the only one who is going to write in the field notebook?

7. I _____ show the class my favorite hiking trail.

8. The students _____ let the rain bother them.

9. He _____ be happy on the trip. He doesn't like camping.

Column B

a. am going to
b. are going to
c. is going to
d. am not going to
e. aren't going to
f. isn't going to
g. are
h. is
i. am

B Write sentences with *will* using the words in parentheses.

1. (we / go / Europe /sometime) _____ *We'll go to Europe sometime.* _____

2. (I / pack / your duffle bag / tonight) _____

3. (He / not / be / late) _____

4. (They / sleep / in / tents) _____

5. (She / buy / a new flashlight / for the trip) _____

6. (It / be / cold / in the mountains) _____

7. (My parents / drive / the van) _____

8. (you / need / rain gear) _____

C Write a question with *be going to* or *will* for the answers given. Use the following question words: *who, why, how, what, when, where.*

1. _____ *Who's going to plan the trip?* _____

Abdul's going to plan the trip.

2. _____

He's going to pack <u>rain gear, a sleeping bag, a flashlight, and binoculars</u>.

3. _____

They're going to pick you up at <u>6:00 AM</u>.

4. _____

<u>Bob's</u> going to come with us.

5. _____

We're going to go <u>to the desert</u>.

6. _____

<u>I don't have room</u> in my duffel bag for a headlamp.

7. _____

We will come home in <u>two weeks</u>.

8. _____

We're <u>going to drive a van</u> to the state park.

D Write a question with the words in parentheses. Then write a short answer for the question given.

1. (you / write / to me) _____ *Will you write to me?* _____
   Yes, _____ *I will.* _____

2. (your parents / go camping / with you) _____?
   No, _____.

3. (your son / take / an extra headlamp) _____?
   Yes, _____.

4. (we / want / to return / in two weeks) _____?
   No, _____.

5. (you / write / in your field journal) _____?

Yes, _____.

E Write a question with the words in parentheses and *be going to*. Then write a short answer for the question given.

1. (you / bring a cooler) _____ *Are you going to bring a cooler?* _____

   No, _____ *I'm not going to.* _____.

2. (the tour guide / talk / with us) _____?

   Yes, _____.

3. (we / leave early) _____?

   No, _____.

4. (they / use / rock hammers / on the trip) _____?

   Yes, _____.

5. (you / pack / today) _____?

   No, _____.

PART TWO   *Be Going To vs. Will:* Uses

A Decide whether each sentence below is a plan, prediction, offer, or promise.

1. He's going to leave tomorrow. _____ *plan* _____

2. It'll be hard to get up early enough. _____

3. Wendy will set her alarm for us. _____

4. I won't forget to pack my flashlight. Don't worry! _____

5. The sun isn't going to come out. _____

6. Len told me he'll drive. _____

7. We'll study for the test next week. _____

8. I'll bring the rain gear this time. Relax! _____

9. We're going to have so much fun. _____

10. The students are going to use rock hammers. _____

B For each question, write an answer as if you were going on a field trip to Mexico. (Answers will vary.)

1. How are you going to get to Mexico?

    I'm going to fly to Mexico.

2. How do you think the trip will turn out?

    _____

3. What will you pack in your duffel bag?

    _____

4. Who is going to go with you?

    _____

5. When will you leave?

    _____

6. Who are you going to miss while you're gone?

    _____

C Make plans, predictions, offers, and promises. Write true sentences about yourself, friends, or family.

Two plans

1. ___ *I am going to the park this weekend.* ___

2. _____

Two predictions

1. _____

2. _____

Two offers

1. _____

2. _____

Two promises

1. _____

2. _____

A **Circle the correct answer to complete the sentence.**

1. Tomorrow night, everyone _____ in tents.

   (a.) sleeps   b. was sleeping   c. were sleeping

2. We _____ at 6:00 in the morning.

   a. leaves   b. leave   c. were leaving

3. Zara _____ an appointment later today.

   a. was having   b. have   c. has

4. I _____ with the group earlier tonight.

   a. met   b. meets   c. meet

5. The students _____ a test next class.

   a. take   b. took   c. takes

6. The kids _____ up at 7:00 AM, we all eat, and then we go.

   a. wake   b. wakes   c. are waking

B **Write a sentence in the present progressive for the future using the words in parentheses.**

1. (Sarah / start / class / tomorrow)

   _____ Sarah's starting class tomorrow. _____

2. (I / go / to the store / at 8:00)

   _____

3. (The buses / arrive / soon)

   _____

4. (You / not come / with us)

   _____

5. (Ben / leave / for the Grand Canyon / next week)

   _____

6. (We / take / a break / later tonight)

   _____

C Complete the conversations with the simple present or present progressive.

1. Maddox: (leave) _____Do you leave_____ next week or the week after?

   Shiloh: We _____are leaving_____ next week.

2. Jennifer: (take) _____ a break later?

   Bradley: No, I _____.

3. James: (start) _____ work soon?

   Jessica: They _____ in a week.

4. Alicia: (begin) _____ the movie at 8:00?

   Angela: Yes, we _____.

5. Carola: (wake up) _____ at 7:00 AM?

   Bruno: Yes, she _____.

D Write sentences about your future plans with the present progressive.

1. _____ I'm going on a family vacation next week. _____

2. _____

3. _____

4. _____

5. _____

E Write sentences about your schedule with the simple present.

1. _____ I finish school next week. _____

2. _____

3. _____

4. _____

5. _____

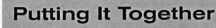

Putting It Together

■ GRAMMAR

A Rewrite the sentences that have mistakes. If there are no mistakes, write "C."

1. The professor are going to give us a test.

   The professor is going to give us a test.

2. We will be going to hike.

   _____

3. I won't probably go today.

   _____

4. She thinks it'll be interesting.

   _____

5. I promise I'm not going to be late.

   _____

6. The show ends at midnight.

   _____

7. What you are doing tomorrow night?

   _____

8. When do you leave for Mexico?

   _____

■ VOCABULARY

Place each vocabulary word in the grid below.

3 letters	7 letters	9 letters	11 letters	13 letters
VAN	CAMPING	DUFFEL BAG	SLEEPING BAG	FIELD NOTEBOOK
	DAY PACK			

4 letters	6 letters	8 letters	10 letters
TENT	COOLER	RAIN GEAR	BINOCULARS
		HEADLAMP	FLASHLIGHT
			ROCK HAMMER

I. Writing a Good Paragraph

A **Read the information below.**

A good paragraph is made up of the following:

- A **topic sentence** is a short sentence that includes the main idea for the paragraph.
- **Supporting sentences** give facts and descriptions to show that the main point of a paragraph is true. Supporting sentences are clearly connected to the topic sentence.
- A **concluding sentence.** This sentence summarizes the paragraph.

B **Read the paragraph below. Write the topic sentence, supporting sentences, and the concluding sentence.**

Mozart

*Wolfgang Amadeus Mozart **was** a great composer. He **was** born on January 27, 1756, in Salzburg, Austria. His father **was** a composer and author of books about music. He **taught** Mozart about music. Mozart **was** only three years old when they **began** their lessons. His father quickly **saw** that Mozart **had** a lot of talent. When Mozart **was** six years old, he **wrote** five pieces for the piano. He **composed** his first symphony when he was eight years old! During his life, Mozart **created** six hundred pieces of music, but he **didn't earn** very much money. He **died** poor on December 5, 1791, at the age of 35. After he died, people realized what a great talent Mozart was.*

1. Topic sentence: _____

2. Supporting sentences:

   a. _____

   b. _____

   c. _____

   d. _____

3. Concluding sentence: _____

C **Choose the best supporting sentences for the following topic sentences.**

1. Beethoven was a courageous composer.
   a. He continued writing music even after he went deaf.
   b. He worked together with Haydn.

2. The cities of the past were very different from the cities of today.
   a. For example, in the Middle Ages, cities were very small.
   b. New York was a Dutch colony.
3. The geology of the Earth is always changing.
   a. The Earth is one of eight planets in the solar system.
   b. There used to be one continent called Pangaea.

II. Writing a Paragraph

A **Take notes in the chart about a famous person.**

Famous Person	(Example: Mozart)
Details	(Example: Born in Salzburg, Austria)

B **Write a topic sentence and a concluding sentence about your famous person.**

1. Topic sentence: _____

2. Concluding sentence: _____

III. Write a paragraph about your famous person.

C Check your paragraph. Use the checklist.

	Yes	No
Topic sentence		
Supporting sentences		
Concluding sentence		
Grammar from lessons 1–10		

D Rewrite your paragraph.

Future Time Clauses: *After/Before/When/As Soon As;* Future Conditional with *If* Clauses; Future Progressive

PART ONE	Future Time Clauses: *After/Before/When/As Soon As*

A **Complete the sentences using the correct form of the word in parentheses.**

Christina: As soon as it _____stops_____ (stop) snowing, I _____'ll walk_____ (walk) home.

Anna: You can't walk home! After we _____ (finish) breakfast, I _____ (ask) my dad to drive you.

Christina: Thanks. Are you going to come, too?

Anna: I don't know. It's freezing outside.

Christina: We _____ (wear) our coats when we _____ (go).

Anna: No, I _____ (not go) with you when you _____ (leave). I'll go later. Can you give me directions to your house?

Christina: Yes. As soon as you _____ (get) to the end of the driveway, you _____ (make) a left. After you _____ (do) that, you _____ (come) to a stop sign. When you _____ (reach) the stop sign, you _____ (not turn). You'll go straight. After you _____ (arrive) at the first stoplight, you _____ (turn) right. Before you _____ (get) to the end of the road, you _____ (see) my house. It's the white one on the left.

Anna: Thanks. Is your family expecting you?

Christina: No, they're not. When they _____ (see) me, they _____ (be) surprised. They think I'm coming home tomorrow.

Anna: That's great. I'll get my dad now.

B **Rewrite the sentences that have mistakes. If there are no mistakes, write "C."**

1. When Bill got to class he'll take a test.

   _____*When Bill gets to class, he'll take a test.*_____

2. The students will leave, as soon as it stops raining.

_____

3. The rain won't stop before we have to leave.

_____

4. You'll finish the review before time will run out.

_____

5. After the professor will discuss the climate, he predicts tomorrow's weather.

_____

6. As soon as the sun comes out, the temperature will increases.

_____

7. When Judy gets nervous she won't sings.

_____

8. We'll travel south before the weather got too cold.

_____

9. After Sammy and John wake up, they'll play in the snow.

_____

10. I won't run when the rainy season starts.

_____

C Write a sentence about the future using the words in parentheses and a time clause. (Answers will vary.)

1. (it / rain / Sandra / not go / outside)

When it rains, Sandra will not go outside.

2. (you / hand in / the test / class / end)

_____

3. (the class / discuss / hurricanes / they / learn / about / thunderstorms)

_____

4. (I / write / my paper / I / give / it / to / you)

_____

5. (we / visit / the library / we / tour / the cafeteria)

_____

6. (recess / start / children / go / outside)

_____

D **Answer the questions below using a future time clause. Use the words in parentheses in your answers.**

1. Who will give you a party when you graduate?   (my mother)

   _____ *When I graduate, my mother will give me a party.* _____

2. How will Stuart prepare before he takes the test?   (study hard)

   _____

3. What will the professors do as soon as the school
   year ends?   (go on vacation)

   _____

4. Where are we going to go after we finish our work?   (go to the movies)

   _____

5. What will I wear when the weather gets colder?   (a jacket)

   _____

6. Who will teach the class after the instructor retires?   (Ms. Jackson)

   _____

7. How will you feel before you find out your grades?   (nervous)

   _____

PART TWO   **Future Conditional with *If* Clauses**

A **Complete each sentence using the correct form of a verb In the box. Some verbs may be used more than once.**

be	wear	study	go	snow	pick
cry	meet	call	come	hold	take

1. If it ____ *snows* ____ a lot, then we ____ *won't go* ____ to school.

2. If you _____ late, you _____ (not) me.

3. I _____ (not) my jacket if the sun _____ out.

4. If Sonya _____ him, Todd _____ happy.

5. If the photographer _____ a bad picture, you _____ (not) pleased.

6. If the baby_____, I _____ her.

7. If the sun _____ out, we _____ a hike.

8. The professors _____ the school day off if it _____ more than five inches.

9. If Jordan _____ every night, she _____ the top student.

10. If he _____ me, I _____ up the phone.

B Circle the correct answer to complete the sentence.

1. If the hurricane _____ the house will flood.

   a. hits   b. will hit,   (c.) hits,

2. The students will _____ if they want to pass the test.

   a. study   b. are studying   c. study,

3. You will _____ a hat if it's cold outside.

   a. wore   b. wear,   c. wear

4. If it _____ we won't go for a walk.

   a. rains   b. rains,   c. , rains

5. I will hike in the woods _____ the sun is shining.

   a. if   b. , if   c. if,

6. If Alison and Janie don't take an umbrella _____ get wet.

   a. , they is going to   b. , they'll   c. they'll

7. We will hold a review session _____ sign up to come.

   a. , if many students   b. if many students   c. if Betty

8. If the phone _____ Stu will answer it.

   a. rings,   b. rings   c. will ring,

C Finish the sentence in column A by matching it with the correct verb and result in column B.

Column A	Column B
1. If Tom sits out in the sun, _c_	a. there won't be any wind damage.
2. If I'm not hungry, ___	b. I'll show up every day.
3. If you wear sunglasses, ___	c. he is going to get a tan.
4. If Susie is cold, ___	d. we won't have to study that much.
5. If the hurricane doesn't hit, ___	e. your eyes will be protected.
6. If we review our notes every day, ___	f. you won't be able to participate.
7. If the temperature decreases, ___	g. I won't eat anything.
8. If the students pass all their classes, ___	h. it'll get cold too cold to play outside.
9. If I want to keep my job, ___	i. she'll put on a sweater.
10. If you don't attend class, ___	j. they'll graduate.

D Write questions to the answers given.

1. _What are you going to do if it rains tomorrow?_

If it rains tomorrow, <u>I'm not going to go for a walk.</u>

2. _____

I'm going to take <u>my best friend</u> with me if I win a free vacation.

3. _____

<u>I'll go to the Bahamas</u> if I win a free vacation.

4. _____

I'll <u>take the bus to school</u> if my car breaks down.

5. _____

<u>My friends will arrive at 10:00</u> if I invite them to a party that begins at 8:00.

6. _____

<u>I'll take a few weeks off</u> if I lose my job.

A Complete the conversation with the future progressive tense of the words in parentheses.

1.　　Juan:　By the end of the year, I __will be speaking__ (speak) fluent English.

　　Ariana:　That's great. Do you realize that during that time we __will be taking__ (take) many English tests.

2.　　Pablo:　Let's review today's notes. During the next century, the climate

　　　　　　_____ (change) rapidly.

Dominique:　By 2050, the oceans _____ (rise) to record levels.

　　Pablo:　In a few years, scientists _____ (make) plans to decrease climate changes. I hope they're successful.

3.　　Kurt:　In two days, I _____ (not attend) class. During that class, you _____ (learn) about thunderstorms. You'll have to share your notes with me.

Courtney:　No problem. By next week, I _____ (show) you all the lessons you missed.

4.　　Diana:　We should leave soon. In an hour, it _____ (start) to snow.

　　Erica:　Yes, and by then my parents _____ (get) worried.

B Write true sentences about yourself, your family, or your friends using the time expressions in parentheses and future progressive verbs.

1. (by next week) _____

2. (in 12 hours) _____

3. (during the next five years) _____

C Write questions using the words in parentheses. Answer the questions with true statements, using future progressives and time expressions.

1. (go / this weekend)

　　_____ Where will you be going this weekend? _____

　　_____ This weekend, I'll be going to Puerto Rico. _____

2. (live / during the next few years)

_____

_____

3. (not happen / in two years)

_____

_____

4. (not do / by the end of the school year)

_____

_____

5. (emotions / experience / during graduation)

_____

_____

6. (work / in three years)

_____

_____

Putting It Together

■ GRAMMAR

A **Rewrite the sentences that have mistakes. If there are no mistakes, write "C."**

1. As soon as we eats dinner, we'll go to the movies.
   _____ *As soon as we eat dinner, we'll go to the movies.* _____

2. Miguel and Susanna will quiz each other after they will finish studying.

   _____

3. Before it stops raining our basement will flooded.

   _____

4. The professor won't give us anymore tests, after he comes back from vacation.

   _____

5. If the sun comes out Jerome, will goes for a run.

   _____

6. The climate will continues to change if scientists don't do something to stop it.

   _____

7. If we don't exercise, we'll get out of shape.

   _____

8. By next Friday, my classmates will be leaving for home.

   _____

9. In a week, I'll be learn more about weather.

   _____

10. During the next hour you won't be learned about geology.

    _____

B Write four sentences with a time clause about your future plans. Use the following time clauses: *after, before, when, as soon as.*

When I graduate from school, I'll get a job.

1. _____

2. _____

3. _____

4. _____

C Write four sentences with *if* clauses about different weather conditions.

1. _____

2. _____

3. _____

4. _____

Find the words in the puzzle and circle them.

```
H  K  L  F  R  V  T  B  I  H  Y  W  M  Q  A
H  B  H  O  R  R  L  N  V  B  W  R  Y  M  T
U  W  U  R  E  E  C  H  K  D  O  A  L  Q  H
W  V  F  Z  T  R  E  X  N  T  D  O  T  K  G
N  S  J  Q  E  W  C  Z  S  I  H  F  E  U
O  X  S  A  M  L  I  N  I  J  U  G  D  G  O
G  E  S  N  O  W  I  N  G  N  I  N  I  A  R
T  E  N  U  M  A  M  V  D  I  G  M  N  P  D
O  T  D  L  R  H  X  E  Q  Y  I  J  U  Y  F
F  Y  E  D  E  C  R  E  A  S  E  G  L  A  N
H  I  O  L  H  S  B  M  V  N  G  Y  P  F  S
L  I  G  H  T  N  I  N  G  H  X  R  H  W  K
Q  D  O  O  L  F  C  N  L  R  U  I  P  P  F
H  U  R  R  I  C  A  N  E  T  L  D  L  T  R
A  M  R  S  C  A  V  Y  N  O  C  Z  G  F  V
```

CLOUDY

DECREASE

DROUGHT

FLOOD

FREEZING

HURRICANE

INCREASE

LIGHTNING

RAINING

RAINSTORM

SNOWING

SUNNY

THERMOMETER

THUNDERSTORM

WINDY

Verbs of Perception: Simple vs. Progressive; Stative Verbs of Emotion/Cognition/Possession

PART ONE	Verbs of Perception: Simple vs. Progressive

A Complete the sentences with the correct form of a verb from the box.

feel	see	look	taste
listen	touch	sound	try

1. This jacket is nice. It _____*feels*_____ so soft.

2. I _____ at some photographs.

3. That music is strange. It _____ so scary.

4. My mother's _____ the sauce to see if it's done.

5. I _____ her car coming around the corner.

6. My sister _____ to the Webcast.

7. Indian food _____ delicious.

8. The tide is high. The waves _____ the rocks.

B Complete the conversations with the right form of the verb in parentheses.

1. Patty: What _____*are*_____ you _____*doing?*_____
                             (do)

   Rula: I _*'m smelling*_ the milk. It _____ bad.
        (smell)   (smell)

   Patty: It _____ OK. Let me _____ it.
          (look)   (taste)

   Rula: Well? How does it _____?
                  (taste)

   Patty: Yuck! It _____ terrible.
            (taste)

2. Abel: What _____ you _____ at? I don't _____ anything.
                         (look)   (see)

     Beth: I'm _____ an eagle.
               (watch)

     Abel: Where?

     Beth: It's up in that tree.

     Abel: Oh, I _____ it. It _____ beautiful!
                (see)   (look)

PART TWO	**Stative Verbs of Emotion/Cognition/Possession**

A Fill in the blanks with the simple present or the progressive.

1. (have) I _____ *have* _____ a large family.

2. (have) We _____ a good time at the party.

3. (know) They _____ us from our old neighborhood.

4. (think) I _____ about all the good times we've had.

5. (want) My parents _____ a new house.

6. (love) My friend Suki _____ learning new languages.

7. (work) We _____ on a new project right now.

8. (try) My brother _____ to find a new job.

9. (not own) We _____ a TV.

10. (have) My daughter _____ difficulty in school now.

B Complete the conversation using the correct form of the word in parentheses.

Lee: What _*are you thinking*_ (think) about?

Leila: I _____ (think) I want to buy a house. _____ (own) your own home?

Lee: Yes. I _____ (have) a condo downtown and a beach house.

Leila: Wow! I _____ (think) that's great! I'm worried about buying something. I _____ (not like) to do all that maintenance!

Lee: I _____ (understand). It's a big responsibility.

Leila: I _____ (believe) owning a home is a good investment, though.

Lee: It is. Property values almost always go up.

Leila: I _____ (need) to talk with a financial advisor.

Lee: That's a good idea. I _____ (know) a really good one.

Leila: Who?

Lee: Me!

Putting It Together

■ GRAMMAR

A Rewrite the sentences that have mistakes. If there are no mistakes, write "C."

1. I'm loving my new gym.   *I love my new gym.*

2. That cheese smells very strong.   _____

3. That coat belongs to my father.   _____

4. I'm thinking he's not home.   _____

5. I believe in a higher power.   _____

6. My boyfriend isn't understanding me. _____

7. They know a great restaurant
   downtown.   _____

8. I'm needing a lot of help right now. _____

9. I feel sick.   _____

10. They have a great time at the
    party tonight.   _____

11. Are you owning a home?   _____

12. I hate not being able to speak Spanish. _____

13. He's hearing music in his bedroom. _____

14. Children like watching parades.   _____

15. The blanket is feeling soft.   _____

B Andrew is talking with Liz on the phone. Correct the mistakes in the underlined words and phrases.

Andrew: Hi, Liz. Where are you?

Liz: I'm in the park.

Andrew: What are you doing?

Liz: I'm watch~~ing~~ my niece and nephew. They're playing.

Andrew: I listen to water.

Liz: Oh, yes. There's a wonderful fountain here. And it's surrounded by beautiful flowers. They are smelling so good.

Andrew: It sounds wonderful.

Liz: Are you hearing the kids laughing and screaming?

Andrew: Yes, they sound happy.

Liz: Well, they certainly are looking happy!

Andrew: Maybe I'm needing to go to the park, too!

Liz: I know what you are meaning!

■ VOCABULARY

Complete the clues to solve the puzzle.

Across

3. There are many _____ performed during a Catholic religious service.

5. Aunts, uncles, and cousins

Down

1. These are what are most important to me in life.

2. We always kiss three times when we meet.

4. conviction

6. Mother, father, and children

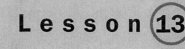

Count Nouns: Singular and Plural Forms; Count vs. Noncount Nouns

PART ONE	Count Nouns: Singular and Plural Forms

A Circle the correct answer to complete the sentences.

1. I have lived in three _____.

   a. cities   b. citys   c. city

2. I will peel and mash five _____ for dinner.

   a. potato   b. potatos   c. potatoes

3. One _____ has to clean the _____.

   a. people / dishs   b. person / dishs   c. person / dishes

4. That baby has just one _____, but I have many _____.

   a. tooth / teeth   b. tooth / toothes   c. teeth / teethes

5. Ivan has two _____ and three _____ on his farm.

   a. cow / pigs   b. cows / pig   c. cows / pigs

6. Betsy has some _____ in her pond and ten _____ in her field.

   a. fishes / sheep   b. fish / sheep   c. fishes / sheeps

7. The school music room has a _____ and some _____.

   a. tuba / pianos   b. tubas / piano   c. tuba / pianoes

8. The cupboard has a lot of _____ for storing many _____ .

   a. shelfs / knifs   b. shelves / knives   c. shelf / knife

9. There are two _____, three _____, and many _____ in the class.

   a. man / woman / children   b. man / womans / children   c. men / women / children

10. Sam gave the cashier one _____, two _____, and three _____.

    a. quarter / pennys /   b. quarter / pennies /   c. quarters / pennies /
       nickels   nickels   nickels

B Complete the sentences by writing the singular or plural form of the nouns in parentheses.

1. A lot of ___*people*___ (person) pay for ___*groceries*___ (grocery) with their credit ___*card*___ (card).

2. A _____ (man) paid for two _____ (apple), three _____ (tomato), and five _____ (box) of spaghetti with cash.

3. Some _____ (child) buy _____ (toy) with the _____ (coin) they find in their pockets.

4. Enrique and Babs have many _____ (belief) about the best way to pay for a _____ (product).

5. Your financial _____ (advisor) will tell you ways to avoid getting into too many money _____ (crisis).

6. We wanted to purchase a _____ (cactus) for our backyard and ended up buying three _____ (cactus) at the plant nursery.

7. Peter and Petra go to two different _____ (church). They listen to several _____ (service) when they go.

8. I saw three _____ (deer) in my backyard yesterday. The smallest _____ was the cutest one.

9. Three _____ (woman) walked into the store to buy a _____ (shirt), two pairs of _____ (shoe), and three _____ (dress).

10. Dorothy introduced me to her three _____ (son) and four _____ (fish).

C Write questions with the words in parentheses. Then answer each question with a singular noun and a plural noun.

1. (What / Frank / buy / at the clothing store)

    _____*What did Frank buy at the clothing store?*_____

    _____*Frank bought one shirt and two pairs of pants at the clothing store.*_____

2. (What / relative / you / invite / to your party)

_____

_____

3. (What / place / we / visit / yesterday)

_____

_____

4. (What / class / Ines / attend / last week)

_____

_____

5. (How many / aunt / and / uncle / you / have)

_____

_____

PART TWO   **Count vs. Noncount Nouns**

A Identify the underlined word in each sentence as a count (C) or noncount (NC) noun.

1. Betty buys her <u>food</u> from the local market.   _____*NC*_____

2. I can't wait to eat this <u>orange</u>.   _____

3. My favorite subject is <u>history</u>.   _____

4. This <u>cheese</u> tastes good.   _____

5. The <u>athletes</u> are exercising.   _____

6. The children are full of <u>energy</u>.   _____

7. We have to finish our <u>homework</u>.   _____

8. Amber bought a beautiful piece of <u>jewelry</u>.   _____

9. You drink two <u>cups</u> of coffee everyday.   _____

10. <u>Economics</u> is an interesting subject.   _____

B Complete the conversation by using the singular or plural form of the nouns in parentheses. Then identify each noun as a count or noncount noun.

Louisa: I love shopping at the ___mall___ (mall).   ___C___

Selena: I saw some _____ (jewelry) at the last store
that I would like to buy.   _____

Louisa: I saw one _____ (necklace) that I liked.   _____

Selena: That store had at least three _____ (ring)
I would wear.   _____

Louisa: If you purchased every item you liked, you would
spend all your _____ (money) in a week.   _____

Selena: Before we leave, I need to pick up some
_____ (milk).   _____

Louisa: That's fine. I'll buy some meat and _____
(vegetable).   _____

Selena: I will also buy some _____ (fruit) like
oranges and grapefruits.   _____

Louisa: Let's go to the kitchen supply _____ (store) next.   _____

Selena: Look. What do you think of these drinking
_____ (glass)?   _____

Louisa: I like them. What about these _____ (knife)?   _____

Selena: They look cheap. I don't think they would cut
_____ (cheese).   _____

Louisa: Do you want to price some _____ (furniture)
before we go to the grocery store?   _____

Selena: Sure. I was thinking about buying some
new _____ (couch) for my living room.   _____

Louisa: I am trying to find new _____ (chair)
for my kitchen.   _____

Selena: Don't get ones with wooden _____ (seat).
Let's find some covered in fabric.   _____

Louisa: Yes. Seats covered in _____ (cotton) might be nice.   _____

Selena: Let's go.

C Make a grocery list using count and noncount nouns. Include the number of count items and specify whether you want *some* or *a lot* of the noncount items.

1. _four bananas_
2. _____
3. _____
4. _____
5. _____
6. _____
7. _____
8. _____
9. _____
10. _____
11. _____
12. _____

Putting It Together

GRAMMAR

Identify the underlined words as count or noncount nouns. If the word is a count noun, write *a/an* with the singular form and a number with the plural form. If the word is a noncount noun, write *some* with the noun. Write *X* if there is no form.

1. I gather all kinds of <u>information</u> on the Internet.

   Singular _____X_____   Plural _____X_____   Noncount _some information_

2. The students bought many <u>pencils</u> at the office supply store.

   Singular _a pencil_   Plural _ten pencils_   Noncount _____X_____

3. Sylvie's pajamas are made of <u>silk</u>.

   Singular _____   Plural _____   Noncount _____

4. Why are you hopping on one <u>foot</u>?

   Singular _____   Plural _____   Noncount _____

5. I bought a nice <u>umbrella</u> today.

   Singular _____   Plural _____   Noncount _____

6. Don't put too much <u>sugar</u> in your coffee.

   Singular _____   Plural _____   Noncount _____

7. Have you met John's <u>wife</u>, Nona?

   Singular _____   Plural _____   Noncount _____

8. The girl's <u>hero</u> is her mother.

   Singular _____   Plural _____   Noncount _____

9. Who are those people in the <u>photo</u>?

   Singular _____   Plural _____   Noncount _____

10. The professor enjoys going to <u>work</u> everyday.

   Singular _____   Plural _____   Noncount _____

11. The <u>roof</u> of that house is gray.

   Singular _____   Plural _____   Noncount _____

12. What <u>company</u> employs your father?

   Singular _____   Plural _____   Noncount _____

■ **VOCABULARY**

Use the clues to solve the puzzle.

Across

3. to bring in from another country

5. The car is a form of _____.

7. to ship to other countries

Down

1. I want to _____ my gift for something else.

2. money gained from the sale of goods

4. to buy and sell goods for other goods

6. physical or mental work

Units of Measure; *Much/ Many/A Lot Of; A Few vs. Few/ A Little vs. Little/Very vs. Too*

PART ONE	Units of Measure

A Circle the correct quantity expression to complete the sentence.

1. Ariel drank _____ coffee this morning.

   a. a bowl of   (b.) a cup of   c. a carton of

2. I roasted _____ chicken with garlic and butter.

   a. a piece of   b. a slice of   c. a gram of

3. Frank had _____ juice with his breakfast.

   a. a glass of   b. a carton of   c. a jar of

4. The professor had _____ sugar in his tea.

   a. a bottle of   b. a can of   c. a teaspoon of

5. We bought _____ pickles to eat as a snack.

   a. a bunch of   b. a jar of   c. a bag of

6. Can you put _____ mustard and _____ milk on the table?

   a. a head of / a cup of   b. a gallon of / a gallon of   c. a bottle of / a carton of

7. The recipe calls for _____ butter and _____ flour.

   a. a cup of / a stick of   b. a stick of / a cup of   c. a pound of / a jar of

8. You cooked _____ bread and _____ meat for dinner.

   a. a bunch of / a   b. a loaf of / a slice of   c. a loaf of / a pound of
   gram of

9. _____ nuts and _____ soda hit the spot.

   a. A package of /   b. A head of / a cup of   c. A cup of / a bag of
   a can of

10. Jerome purchased _____ lettuce and _____ carrots for his salad.

    a. a gram of / a box of b. a head of / a bunch of c. a piece of / a gram of

B Complete the sentences by filling in the blanks with quantity expressions.

1. Darlene puts two ___*teaspoons of*___ sugar in her coffee.

2. The boy was allowed to have three _____ candy after dinner.

3. The doctor said that forty _____ fat per day is too much.

4. It takes me a week to finish a ___ _____ cereal and a _____ yogurt.

5. How come there are three _____ jam and four _____ cheese in the refrigerator?

6. We shared two _____ cocoa and a _____ cake for dessert.

7. The soccer team ate 40 _____ pizza and drank five _____ water during their celebration dinner.

8. Would you like a _____ water or a _____ pretzels?

9. Stacey needed three _____ sugar, two _____ butter, and four _____ flour to make her cookies.

10. The salad was so big I used two _____ lettuce, one _____ carrots, and a _____ celery.

11. My mother asked me to buy two _____ bread, a _____ bananas, and a _____ milk at the grocery store.

C Write true answers to the questions below. Be sure to use a quantity expression in your answer.

1. How much pizza do you usually eat in one sitting?
   _____*I usually eat five slices of pizza in one sitting.*_____

2. How much water do you drink everyday?
   _____

3. Do you like to have bread with every meal?
   _____

4. What is your favorite snack food?

_____

5. What are some foods that are typically in your refrigerator?

_____

6. Do you keep food in your cupboards?

_____

A Circle the nouns following *much, many,* and *a lot of.* Then indicate whether each noun is a count (C) or noncount (NC).

1. Too many (people) have birthdays in July.   _____C_____

2. How many days until your birthday?   _____

3. Betty ate too much ice cream on her last birthday.   _____

4. Do you eat a lot of sugar on your birthday?   _____

5. A lot of children have parties on their birthdays.   _____

6. There aren't a lot of adults who like to celebrate
   with parties.   _____

7. Is there much purpose in celebrating getting older?   _____

8. Do you invite a lot of friends over on your birthday?   _____

9. I don't like a lot of noise on my birthday.   _____

10. Sally didn't get much jewelry for her birthday.   _____

11. Raoul got a lot of money on his special day.   _____

12. My family doesn't celebrate many birthdays in December.   _____

13. How much cake do you usually eat at parties?   _____

14. Are there many calories in one slice of cake?   _____

B Complete the conversation by filling in the blanks with *much, many,* or *a lot of.* In some cases, one or more quantity expressions may be possible.

Diego: I have ____*a lot of*____ classes this semester. I'm afraid the professors
         are going to assign me too _____ homework.

Javier: I haven't spent _____ time in the classroom lately. I'm not sure how _____ help I can offer you, but we can study together.

Diego: Let's talk about it over lunch.

Javier: Our school cafeteria serves too _____ meat. There aren't _____ vegetables on the menu.

Diego: Do you like to eat _____ vegetables?

Javier: Not really. I know you're supposed to eat _____ them.

Diego: How _____ servings are you supposed to eat a day?

Javier: I think you're supposed to eat three to five servings of fruits and vegetables.

Diego: Do you want _____ cheese on your burger?

Javier: Yes, I like _____ cheese.

Diego: Is there too _____ ketchup on it for you?

Javier: No, that looks OK. Let's see how _____ money we owe.

Diego: How _____ money do you have left on your meal card?

Javier: I don't have _____ money left.

Diego: I'll pay this time. I have _____ money left for food.

Javier: Do you want ice cream?

Diego: No, there aren't _____ flavors. I don't like vanilla ice cream.

Javier: There are too _____ people in here.

Diego: Are there _____ places to sit outside?

Javier: Yes, let's eat out there.

C Write questions with the words in parentheses using *much, many,* and *a lot of*. Then write answers that are true for you.

1. (cheese / eat / everyday)

   _____ How much cheese do you eat every day? _____
   _____ I eat two slices of cheese every day. _____

2. (serving / of / broccoli / have / in a week)

   _____
   _____

3. (drink / coffee / before noon)

   _____
   _____

4. (sugar / like / with / cereal)

_____

_____

5. (person / know / on a diet)

_____

_____

PART THREE   *A Few* vs. *Few/A Little* vs. *Little/Very* vs. *Too*

A Circle the nouns following (a) *few* and (a) *little*. Then indicate whether each is count or noncount.

1. Nadia enjoys a few (minutes) of sleep before her afternoon class. _____*C*_____

2. Janie gets little sleep the night before a big test. _____

3. The children are encouraged to get a little fresh air each day. _____

4. I missed very few classes this semester. _____

5. The professor gives out few perfect grades. _____

6. The students spend too little time studying. _____

B Complete the sentences with (a) *few* or (a) *little*. Add *very* or *too* when necessary. Indicate whether the sentence expresses a positive (+) or a negative (−) quantity.

1. It isn't healthy that Anastasia eats _____*few*_____ vegetables. _____−_____

2. Dirk surprised his girlfriend with _____ pieces of jewelry. _____

3. My nutritionist wants me to eat _____ protein at each meal. _____

4. A can of soda has _____ nutritional value. _____

5. My five-year-old nephew has celebrated _____ birthdays. _____

6. The cafeteria supplies _____ nutritional information. _____

C Write sentences by using the words in parentheses and adding (a) *few* or (a) *little*.

1. (the doctor / want / me / eat / fat)

   The doctor wants me to eat little fat.

2. (Omar / have / carrot / every night / with dinner)

   _____

3. (my father / put / sugar / in his tea)

   _____

4. (the students / get / minutes / in between classes)

   _____

5. (We / have / money / between / the two of us)

   _____

Putting It Together

GRAMMAR

A Rewrite the sentences that have mistakes. If there are no mistakes, write "C."

1. We had ten pounds of pizza for dinner. _We had ten slices of pizza for dinner._

2. I like to eat a stick of toast in the morning. _____

3. Andy added two cup of sugar to his coffee. _____

4. Nona ate two fruits for lunch. _____

5. Too many moneys isn't always a good thing. _____

6. Are there much calories in a candy bar? _____

7. There isn't a lot of time to study for the test. _____

8. Do you eat very much vegetables? _____

9. I have seen very little movies lately. _____

10. The children eat too few protein. _____

11. David has few knowledge about
    economics.

    _____

12. He takes a little sugar in his coffee.   _____

B **Read the following sentences and note which quantity expression is used in each: *much, many, few,* or *little.* Then rewrite the sentences without changing their meaning by choosing another quantity expression from *much, many, few,* or *little.***

1. Linda wears little makeup on her face.

   Linda doesn't wear much makeup on her face.

2. I don't have just a few friends.

   _____

3. Sam doesn't have much time to study.

   _____

4. Elena puts too many books in her backpack.

   _____

5. We didn't have many tests this week.

   _____

6. Abdul had a few pieces of candy.

   _____

C **Write four sentences that are true for you using *much* or *many.***

   I have many friends to call this weekend.

1. _____

2. _____

3. _____

4. _____

D **Write four sentences that are true for you using *few* or *little.***

   I make little time to exercise.

1. _____

2. _____

3. _____

4. _____

■ VOCABULARY

Use the clues to solve the puzzle.

Across

4. rice, wheat, pasta

5. butter, oil

6. milk, cheese, yogurt

Down

1. lettuce, carrots

2. bananas, peaches

3. meat, tofu

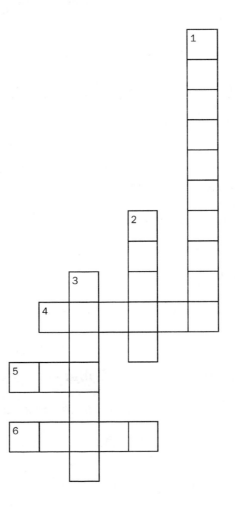

Quantity: *Some/Any/No/None;* General vs. Specific: Articles and Quantity Expressions; *Some/Others/One/ Another/Other/The Other/The Others*

PART ONE	Quantity: *Some/Any/No/None*

A Indicate whether *some, any, no,* or *none* in each sentence below is being used as an adjective (A) or pronoun (P).

Jacob:	The professor didn't give us any homework today.	*A*
Leslie:	That's great. My history professor did give me some homework.	_____
	Do you know where I can get any information about ancient Rome?	_____
Jacob:	I have no books about ancient Rome in my dorm room.	_____
Leslie:	Are you sure you have none?	_____
Jacob:	Yes. Let's try the library. There should be some sources there.	_____
Leslie:	There are sure to be some.	_____
Jacob:	There is no directory showing us where to go.	_____
Leslie:	You're right. There is none.	_____
Jacob:	Let's ask the librarian. Are there any resources on ancient Rome?	_____
Leslie:	Are there any at all?	_____
Jacob:	We can't find any.	_____
Librarian:	You have to go downstairs to find some Roman periodicals.	_____
	Just ask the librarian down there for some help.	_____
Jacob:	Thanks. We'll ask her for some.	_____

B Complete the sentences by filling in the blanks with *some, any, no,* or *none.*

1. The professor has set aside _____*some*_____ classes for language learning.

2. The students will discuss the stages of childhood in _____.

3. The professor doesn't want _____ students to miss these classes.

4. If everyone attends the first class, the professor won't assign _____ homework.

5. The students were thrilled to hear he won't assign _____.

6. Celia had _____ words to express her joy.

7. She had _____.

C Use *any* to write questions with the words in parentheses. Then write answers using *some, any, no,* or *none.*

1. (your classmates / speak / Spanish)

   _____*Do any of your classmates speak Spanish?*_____

   _____*Yes, some of them do.*_____

2. (baby / have / comprehension of language)

   _____

   _____

3. (professor / hand out / too much homework)

   _____

   _____

4. (your classmates / take / English class)

   _____

   _____

5. (your friends / like / to watch / television / in English)

   _____

   _____

6. (infant / communicate / with / their parent)

   _____

   _____

A Indicate whether the sentences below are specific (S) or general (G).

1. The child is babbling. ___S___

2. Babies communicate by babbling and gesturing. _____

3. All of the students passed the test. _____

4. Many students graduate with honors. _____

5. Every mother worries about her children. _____

6. Some people speak several languages. _____

7. Many of the professors have tenure. _____

8. None of the babies cried when their mothers spoke. _____

9. Some of the fathers cried when their children were born. _____

10. Each baby cries to communicate. _____

11. Most of my classmates attend every class. _____

12. No student missed the final exam. _____

13. A mother often teaches her baby about sounds and rhythm. _____

14. Every one of the professors has a college education. _____

15. Most babies recognize their mothers by voice. _____

16. An exam is often difficult. _____

17. I know my brother loves me. _____

18. All tests reinforce what students have learned. _____

19. Each one of the students understood the professor. _____

20. The infants were learning language in stages. _____

B Circle the correct answer to complete the sentence.

1. _____ had trouble recognizing their mother's voice.

   a. None of infants   b. None   c. None of the infants

2. I think _____ are very intelligent.

   a. none children   b. all children   c. no child

3. Why did _____ miss class?

   a. each students   b. some of the students   c. one students

4. _____ imitates the mother's language.

   a. A baby   b. All of the babies   c. Many babies

5. Does _____ know how to talk?

   a. many infants   b. each infant   c. many of the infants

6. _____ can understand intonation.

   a. Every one child   b. Most of children   c. Most of the children

7. Dede thought _____ was hard.

   a. some of the questions   b. each one of the question   c. the question

8. _____ got question five correct.

   a. All of the students   b. No of the students   c. all student

C Fill in the blanks with *a, an, the, some,* or Ø if the sentence does not need an article or quantity expression.

1. __The__ student has two days to study for the test. He's very nervous.

2. _____ nice children were playing in the park yesterday. I didn't know them.

3. _____ baby feels safe with its mother.

4. _____ infant needs its mother.

5. _____ teachers have to challenge students, or they'll never learn.

6. _____ child learns words on a daily basis.

7. _____ children have bigger vocabularies than others.

8. _____ new vocabulary was difficult for the ESL students.

9. _____ father is like a big kid when playing with his children.

10. _____ tests challenge students.

11. _____ tests are more difficult than others.

D Complete the sentences with your own ideas.

1. All children _____ *like to play.* _____

2. All of the children _____

3. Every adult _____

4. Every one of the adults _____

5. Each instructor _____

6. Each of the instructors _____

7. Most students _____

8. Most of the students _____

9. Many schools _____

10. Many of the schools _____

11. Some children _____

12. Some of the children _____

13. No child _____

14. None of the children _____

PART THREE *Some/Others/One/Another/Other/The Other/The Others*

A Indicate whether *some/others/one/another/other/the other/the others* in the sentences are being used as adjectives (A) or pronouns (P).

1. One student asked a question about child development. ___A___

2. One asked about the upcoming test. _____

3. Another student asked a question about language. _____

4. Another answered the question about language. _____

5. Other students were discussing the lesson. _____

6. Others were talking about the history of language. _____

7. Some women were shopping at the mall. _____

8. Some were getting coffee at the café. _____

9. The other women were dining in the restaurant. _____

10. The others were sitting at the bar. _____

11. One child wrote on the blackboard. _____

12. The other sat quietly in his seat. _____

B Complete the sentences by filling in the blanks with the correct form of *some/others/one/another/other/the other/the others*. (Answers may vary.)

The classroom was busy today. _____*Some*_____ students were studying alone. _____ were reviewing the lesson in small groups. The professor helped _____ person find information in the textbook. The teacher's assistant helped _____ use the computer to locate the answer. Three of the students stayed after class ended _____ _____ students headed to their next classes. _____ went to the cafeteria. The meal choices in the cafeteria included cheeseburgers and garden salads. _____ choice included lasagna and bread. _____ included fresh fruit and yogurt. _____ classmate selected a salad. _____ classmate picked the fruit and yogurt. _____ decided to eat somewhere else.

C Complete the sentences below with remarks that are true for you.

1. Some of my family members _____*live in Italy.*_____

   Others _____*live in the United States.*_____

2. My other family members _____

   The others _____

3. One of my friends _____

   The other _____

4. Some of my teachers _____

   Others _____

5. One of my classes _____

   Another _____

■ **GRAMMAR**

A Rewrite the sentences that have mistakes. If there are no mistakes, write "C."

1. Lisa and Wilfred played with some ball.   *Lisa and Wilfred played with a ball.*

2. They left somes in the bag.   _____

3. There is no written history about the school.   _____

4. I doesn't have any idea what the answer is.   _____

5. Are there any evidence that she is correct?   _____

6. Each men learn how to use tools.   _____

7. Many of infants participated in the study.   _____

8. I think the children are babbling.   _____

9. None information is correct.   _____

10. One baby is taking a bath.   _____

11. Other baby were crawling on the floor.   _____

12. Another mothers watched her baby clap.   _____

13. Two other were babbling.   _____

14. Every sugar is bad for you.   _____

15. The babies can understand intonation.   _____

16. The book will never be replaced by computers.   _____

B **Write four sentences about the customs of your native country. Use the words in parentheses.**

Some of the children in my home country speak both Quechua and Spanish.

1. (some) _____

2. (others) _____

3. (one) _____

4. (another) _____

5. (other) _____

6. (the other) _____

7. (the others) _____

■ VOCABULARY

Place each vocabulary word in the grid below.

6 letters	7 letters	9 letters	10 letters	13 letters
BABBLE	GESTURE	REINFORCE	CONSONANTS	COMPREHENSION
RHYTHM	IMITATE	RECOGNIZE	INTONATION	
STAGES				
VOWELS				

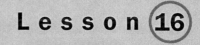
Adjectives and Adverbs; Participial Adjectives; Nouns as Adjectives

---

PART ONE   Adjectives and Adverbs

A **Read through the following conversation. Circle the adjectives. Underline the adverbs.**

Jin: Mr. Dixon is a (good) teacher. He's <u>especially</u> good at explaining (tough) concepts.

Suki: I agree. He's very patient.

Jin: Sometimes his tests are pretty hard. I didn't find the last test easy. I felt like I was working through the problems very slowly.

Suki: I worked through the test quickly. But before the test I met with Mr. Dixon for a personal review session.

Jin: Maybe I will do that next time. I'm a bit impatient when it comes to studying.

Suki: Let's study together. We can work through all the review questions carefully.

Jin: OK. That's a good idea.

B **Identify whether the underlined words are adjectives (adj.) or adverbs (adv.). If the word is an adjective, rewrite it as an adverb. If the word is an adverb, rewrite it as an adjective.**

1. I am a <u>hard-working</u> person.   _adj., hard worker_

2. Sandy cares <u>passionately</u> for animals.   _____

3. Kevin worked <u>fast</u>.   _____

4. The nurse is <u>patient</u>.   _____

5. The doctor is <u>busy</u>.   _____

6. We <u>politely</u> held the doors.   _____

7. The baby was <u>careful</u> when first
   walking.   _____

8. The boy <u>quickly</u> ran to his mom.   _____

9. They are <u>ambitious</u> workers.   _____

C Complete the sentences using the adjectives and adverbs in the boxes. Each word
will be used once.

calm	sudden	careful	well	skillfully
good	rationally	impolite	slowly	punctual

1. The accountant has to be _____*careful*_____ when dealing with numbers.

2. I walked _____ down the street so I could look in all the shop
   windows.

3. Gisella handled the problem _____.

4. His _____ manner put us all at ease.

5. Dirk does _____ in all his classes and expects to graduate with
   honors.

6. I'm   at communicating my ideas to others.

7. The professor is always _____, so we were surprised when he
   showed up late the other day.

8. The girl's _____ answer made her mother mad.

9. The talented doctor _____ mended the broken bone.

10. Donna's _____ announcement surprised all of us.

D List six adjectives that describe you.

1. _____   3. _____   5. _____

2. _____   4. _____   6. _____

E List the six adjectives you used to describe yourself in their adverb forms
(if possible).

1. _____   3. _____   5. _____

2. _____   4. _____   6. _____

A Circle the participial adjectives in the sentences below. Then decide whether the adjective is describing how the modified noun is feeling (F) or whether it's describing a characteristic (C) of the modified noun.

1. Inez is (excited) about choosing her career path.   _f_

2. She wants to find a job that is challenging.   _____

3. Her mother is interested to see what she picks.   _____

4. I want to start an interesting career.   _____

5. Doesn't everyone want a fascinating job?   _____

6. Are you bored by any of your classes?   _____

7. The professor tried motivating the students.   _____

8. He was satisfied with the results of the exam.   _____

9. Don't be depressed if you don't do well in every course. _____

10. It's not surprising that most students don't do well in every course.   _____

B Choose the correct form of the participial adjectives in the following sentences.

It's (amazed/amazing) that more people don't work from home. I'm (surprised/surprising) that more employees don't quit their office jobs and work from their home offices. I can't think of a more (compelled/compelling) way to earn money. Aren't you (interested/interesting) in working while still wearing your pajamas? Don't you wish you never had to deal with another (annoyed/annoying) coworker? You probably have to be a (motivated/motivating) person to be successful at working at home. Don't be (worried/worrying) about not earning enough money. My earnings are competitive. If you do start working from home, you'll never feel more (relaxed/relaxing).

C Complete the sentences by using the participial adjective form of the verbs in the boxes. Each word will be used once.

confuse	relax	disappoint	terrify	concern
entertain	amuse	bore	interest	tire

1. Stefan had a _____terrifying_____ nightmare last night.

2. I am _____ about which career path I should take.

3. Katrina's _____ desk job keeps her looking for a new career.

4. We are so _____ of having to wake up every morning at 6:00 AM.

5. They always watch that _____ television show that comes on at 9:00 PM.

6. Diana was _____ in learning more about being a surgeon.

7. Why are you so _____ at my clumsiness?

8. It was unfortunate the results of the exam were so _____.

9. Don't be _____ about things you can't control.

10. Why don't you sit and listen to the _____ music?

PART THREE   Nouns as Adjectives

A **Identify the noun phrases and the nouns they describe in the following sentences.**

1. Alanna attends three classes at her community college.

   noun phrase _____community_____   noun _____college_____

2. I just got a job at the car dealership on Fifth Avenue.

   noun phrase _____   noun _____

3. Mr. Broverman is a history teacher.

   noun phrase _____   noun _____

4. Sal recently started a low-carbohydrate diet.

   noun phrase _____   noun _____

5. The 4-month-old baby uses crying to communicate.

   noun phrase _____   noun _____

6. How did the meeting with your career counselor go?

   noun phrase _____   noun _____

7. Her mother made a garden salad for lunch.

   noun phrase _____   noun _____

8. All the students attended the championship game.

noun phrase _____   noun _____

B **Complete the sentences with a noun phrase and the noun they describe.**

1. A professor who teaches economics is an *economics teacher* .

2. When you list a profile of your personality online, you have a
   _____.

3. A student who attends nursing school is a _____.

4. When you've created a plan for the next five years, you have a
   _____.

5. When you've made a choice about your career, you've made a
   _____.

6. Ice cream that is flavored with strawberries is _____.

7. A field where football is played is a _____.

8. An assistant to an editor is an _____.

Putting It Together

GRAMMAR

A **Rewrite the sentences that have mistakes. If there are no mistakes, write "C."**

1. Lila is hardworking, calmly, and polite.   *Lila is hardworking, calm, and polite.*

2. We were quiet working in the library.   _____

3. Do you think the professor teaches good?   _____

4. Darrell feels irritating when he's
   running late.   _____

5. Are you surprised that he showed
   up on time?   _____

6. The keynote speaker was very
   motivating.   _____

7. The 25-years-old student is ready
   to graduate.   _____

8. Did you meet the English teacher? _____

9. The cars mechanic is very good at his job. _____

B Write four sentences describing someone you know. Be sure to use adjectives and adverbs.

_____ *My best friend is very interesting.* _____

1. _____

2. _____

3. _____

4. _____

C Write four sentences that are true for you using participial adjectives.

_____ *I am very excited about graduating.* _____

1. _____

2. _____

3. _____

4. _____

D Use nouns from column A and column B to create sentences with noun phrases and the nouns they describe.

Column A	Column B
history	technician
state	work
computer	teacher
field	student
graduate	school

1. _____ *My history teacher is very intelligent.* _____

2. _____

3. _____

4. _____

5. _____

Find the words in the puzzle and circle them.

```
V  U  T  J  O  T  S  C  Q  V  W  C  S  O  I
R  T  J  H  Y  S  N  O  B  H  O  Y  X  S  Y
C  A  R  E  E  R  H  M  E  O  G  O  Y  D  F
U  J  U  B  Y  X  G  P  P  Z  X  K  T  W  R
C  H  A  R  A  C  T  E  R  I  S  T  I  C  S
T  O  C  A  T  D  R  T  S  U  S  L  L  D  S
I  N  M  A  B  A  B  I  F  U  S  A  A  E  A
P  M  E  M  T  I  K  T  O  M  K  N  N  P  N
U  A  P  I  U  A  H  I  F  Y  I  O  O  E  O
N  B  V  O  C  N  T  V  V  T  L  I  S  N  I
C  E  C  O  L  I  I  E  W  J  L  T  R  D  T
T  H  G  D  B  I  F  C  T  W  S  A  E  E  O
U  P  L  M  G  M  T  F  A  S  J  R  P  N  M
A  W  A  N  X  B  C  E  E  T  J  I  H  T  E
L  H  F  T  N  E  D  N  E  P  E  D  N  I  R
```

AMBITIOUS

CAREER

CHARACTERISTICS

COMMUNICATE

COMPETITIVE

COOPERATIVE

DEPENDENT

EFFICIENT

EMOTIONAL

IMPOLITE

INDEPENDENT

PERSONALITY

POLITE

PUNCTUAL

RATIONAL

SKILLS

PART ONE	**Gerunds and Gerund Phrases**

A Circle the gerunds and gerund phrases in the sentences below. Then write S if the gerund is a subject and O if the gerund is an object.

1. (Finding the perfect outfit) for a date is difficult.   *S*

2. I enjoy running five miles a day.   ____

3. Shopping is a fun activity.   ____

4. We will go hiking tomorrow.   ____

5. Do you like getting advice from your parents?   ____

6. Talking to strangers is hard.   ____

7. The professor suggested reviewing for the test.   ____

8. Interviewing for a job makes Jose nervous.   ____

B Circle the correct form of the verbs to complete the sentences.

1. The students _____ careers in the medical field.

   a. considered entering   b. considering entering   c. considered entered

2. _____ a career path is frustrating.

   a. Not have   b. Not having   c. Not haves

3. Omer enjoys _____ at the gym.

   a. to work out   b. working out   c. works out

4. Can we _____ at the lake?

   a. going fishing   b. goes fishing   c. go fishing

5. The chef _____ meat thoroughly.

   a. recommending cooking   b. recommended cooks   c. recommends cooking

6. Ashley avoids _____ fatty foods.

   a. eats   b. eating   c. to eat

7. We can't imagine _____ after all this time in school.

   a. graduating   b. graduated   c. to graduate

8. _____ careers is difficult.

   a. Changing   b. Changes   c. Changed

C Complete the sentences using the correct forms of the verbs in the boxes. Each pair will be used once.

suggest/work	risk/lose	go/sail	avoid/interview	practice/deal
recommend/attend	involve/teach	consider/give	discuss/improve	miss/take

1. The professor and I _discussed improving_ my grades.

2. Stefan loves to _____ in the ocean.

3. My career counselor _____ in a doctor's office.

4. Part of an education student's schooling _____ classes.

5. Do you _____ your university now that you've graduated?

6. Isaiah _____ Grammar 101 before English 101.

7. Don't _____ for jobs just because you're nervous.

8. I think you should _____ with difficult questions.

9. How can you _____ such a great job?

10. The professor _____ the test next week.

PART TWO   **Verbs + Infinitives; Verbs + Infinitives or Gerunds**

A Circle the verbs, underline the infinitives or gerunds, and double underline any objects in the following sentences. Indicate whether the underlined words are infinitives *(I)* or gerunds *(G)*.

1. Sonny (decided) to run in the park.   _I_

2. You seem to be upset about your grade.   _____

3. We refused to give out our phone numbers. _____

4. Wayne's teammate chose him to become captain. _____

5. I enjoy talking on the phone. _____

6. The doctor advised his patient to take the medication. _____

7. Vera taught her daughter to speak English. _____

8. The manager hired Katerina to work the nightshift. _____

9. I expect to graduate from college next spring. _____

10. My father expects me to graduate from college this winter. _____

11. We love listening to music in the evening. _____

12. I can't stand to be left alone at night. _____

13. They persuaded me to call out of work. _____

14. Hans remembered working last Tuesday. _____

15. The professor forgot to remind the class about the test. _____

B Complete the conversation by filling in the blanks with the correct form of the verbs in parentheses. Add nouns or pronouns if necessary.

Emilio: What do you (hope / achieve) ___*hope to achieve*___ working for a company like this?

Lin: I (want / experience) _____ a positive work environment that will be a good place for me to learn and grow.

Emilio: I (want / remind) _____ you that our goal as a company (be / hire) _____ motivated employees.

Lin: I (consider myself / be) _____ self-motivated and hardworking.

Emilio: We (prefer / employ) _____ workers that have those characteristics.

What else can you tell us about yourself?

Lin: When I was working as a teacher's assistant, I worked with students on their study skills. I (taught / review) _____ the material in a way that would help them succeed when taking exams.

Emilio: I have several other interviews to conduct before I make a decision. I (not able / offer) _____ you a job at this time. Someone from the office will call you in the next week or so.

Lin: Thank you. I (hope / hear) _____ from you soon.

C Complete the sentences by filling in the blanks with the gerund or infinitive form of the words verbs in parentheses.

Wendell usually leaves work by 11:00 PM. But this night he remembered he needed (stop) _____*to stop*_____ at the grocery store before going home. The grocery store closes at 10:30 PM. He stopped (work) _____ and approached his boss about leaving early. Wendell remembered (see) _____ a deer on the side of the road before. So he tried (keep) _____ an eye out in case one jumped into the road. Wendell reminded himself (not forget) _____ pick up the groceries. But in the store, he forgot (check) _____ his grocery list. So he didn't remember (get) _____ everything he needed.

PART THREE	Prepositions Followed by Gerunds

A Complete the sentences with the correct form of the verb in parentheses. Add a preposition if necessary.

1. (study) Most students succeed in school _____*by studying*_____ hard.

2. (clean) I help my parents _____ once a week.

3. (win the lottery) My uncle thinks _____ all the time.

4. (take time off) I believe _____ to stay in shape.

5. (write in English) Carol is good _____.

6. (work with children) Brittany has an interest _____.

7. (speak in public) My son has a talent _____.

8. (see a movie) I look forward _____ every Friday night.

9. (say) _____ no, I want you to think about all the possibilities.

10. (come) _____ home, he sat down to watch TV.

B Complete the sentences with the correct form of a verb in the box. Some verbs may be used more than once.

have	wait	give	take	become
make	Say	decide	speak	shop

1. I left after _____*waiting*_____ 20 minutes.

2. Maria thought for a long time before _____ to get married.

3. I didn't want to go without _____ goodbye.

4. The students weren't used to _____ so much homework.

5. My family is accustomed to _____ vacation together.

6. Angie doesn't care about _____ a lot of money.

7. I look forward to _____ to you at our next meeting.

8. Every week I help my elderly parents with _____.

9. Autistic children are not good at _____ eye contact.

10. I'll never have a chance at _____ a concert pianist.

11. Supermodel Claudia Schiffer has a passion for _____ out against cruelty to animals.

12. Franco believes in _____ to charities.

Putting It Together

GRAMMAR

A **Rewrite the sentences that have mistakes. If there are no mistakes, write "C."**

1. I can't imagine to work as a clown.   *I can't imagine working as a clown.*

2. Effie's dream job is saves lives.   _____

3. To shop is a fun activity.   _____

4. She advised to look at a lot of colleges in the Midwest.   _____

5. They want me to become a doctor.   _____

6. We want us to be happy in our careers?   _____

7. You to need finishing your homework.   _____

8. Adela prefers being honest.   _____

9. Are nurses afraid of to make mistakes?   _____

10. The professor thanked us for work with him.   _____

11. Dora isn't interested in become
    an actress.

    _____

12. I didn't get a chance at succeed
    on the test.

    _____

B Write a question with the words in parentheses in the present tense. Then give a short answer that is true for you.

1. (like / help others)

    _____ Do you like helping others? _____
    _____ Yes, I do. OR No, I don't _____

2. (look forward to / finish classes)

    _____

    _____

3. (expect / have / a job soon)

    _____

    _____

4. (prefer / work / with people)

    _____

    _____

5. (care about / get good grades)

    _____

    _____

6. (afraid of / fail / at work or at school)

    _____

    _____

7. (have a passion for / learn languages)

    _____

    _____

8. (want / learn / another language)

    _____

    _____

C Complete each sentence by adding a gerund or gerund phrase. Write sentences that are true for you.

1. I began _____ *studying English two years ago.* _____

2. I like _____

3. I started _____

4. I enjoy _____

5. I hate _____

D Use the verbs, prepositions, or gerunds in parentheses to write sentences that are true for you.

1. (by writing)

_____ *I learned a lot about English by writing letters.* _____

2. (without thinking)

_____

3. (care about living)

_____

4. (look forward to working)

_____

5. (be familiar with looking)

_____

6. (have a talent for earning)

_____

Unscramble each of the clue words. Copy the letters in the numbered cells to other cells with the same number.

LAOSG

	2		7	

REEDUPSA

	3	10	8		9	

TO NODSECRI

1		11			5	6

OT NEGMAII

				4	

1	2	3	4	5	6

7	8	1	1	9	10	11

Adjectives + Infinitive; *Too/Enough* + Infinitive; Adverbial Infinitives of Purpose: *To/In Order To*

PART ONE   Adjectives + Infinitive

A Read the following sentences. Circle the adjectives and underline the infinitives.

Ms. Watts, the (astronomy) professor, was (disappointed) to note that she could barely see the night sky while on campus. The grounds were well lit at night, so it was almost impossible to spot many stars. Ms. Watts was happy to learn that a nearby field was available for stargazing. She was very excited to see that many students had signed up for her stargazing course. Ms. Watts was eager to show them how the night sky looked under the telescope. She was careful to set up her telescopes to show several different constellations. The students who came were surprised to see so many stars. It was easy to examine them with the low light and powerful equipment.

B Complete the sentences by filling in the blanks with the correct form of the adjective in parentheses.

1. Augustine was a little (afraid) _____afraid_____ to take his final exams.

2. Avia was (eager) _____ to tell her parents she got an A on her paper.

3. It's (surprise) _____ to learn that the sun is a star.

4. We're (excite) _____ to observe the new planet.

5. Is it (possible) _____ to live on another planet?

6. The scientists were (disappoint) _____ to discover their experiment failed.

7. Gravity can be (difficult) _____ to explain.

8. The professor was (surprise) _____ to see that so many students missed yesterday's class.

C Complete the sentences by using the correct form of the adjectives and verbs in the boxes. Each pair should only be used once.

afraid/spend	please/be	careful/damage	excite/learn
possible/live	surprise/hear	easy/understand	disappoint/find out

1. Effie was ___surprised to hear___ the bell indicating that class had ended.

2. The scientists were _____ (not) any specimens in the lab.

3. How is it _____ on a planet so close to the sun?

4. It was _____ the results of the test.

5. I was _____ that I had enough credits to graduate.

6. Why are you _____ any money?

7. It isn't _____ the infinite size of space.

8. The students were _____ enrolled in their classes.

PART TWO *Too/Enough* + Infinitive

A Match each question in column A with the correct answer in column B.

Column A	Column B
1. Why can't humans live under water?	a. It's too hot.
2. Why can't life survive on the sun?	b. There's not enough wind.
3. Why couldn't we see the star?	c. There's too much sand.
4. Why are plants hard to grow in the desert?	d. There's not enough oxygen.
5. Why won't my kite fly?	e. It's too far away.

B Complete the sentences by filling in the blanks with the correct form of the adjective or noun in parentheses and *too* or *enough*. Add *much/many/few/little* as needed.

1. Children are ___too young___ (young) to attend college.

2. Busy people don't have _____ (time) to participate in leisure activities.

3. Is there _____ (oxygen) for us to survive on Mars?

4. A 22-year-old is _____ (old) to pay children's price for the movies.

5. The soup was _____ (cold) for us to eat.

6. There wasn't _____ (water) for all of us to drink.

7. There was _____ (wind) to run today.

8. Is the moon _____ (close) for us to observe?

9. You have _____ (time) to be wasting it on arguing.

10. There were _____ (calories) in that donut.

C Write sentences using the words in parentheses. Be sure to use an infinitive and *too* or *enough*. Add *much/many/few/little* as needed.

1. (Manny / be / young / drive)

   _____ Manny is too young to drive. _____

2. (the professor / not have / time / grade / the test)

   _____

3. (I / have / money / eat out)

   _____

4. (you / not be / old / retire)

   _____

5. (the sun / be / bright / look / directly at it)

   _____

PART THREE   Adverbial Infinitives of Purpose: *To/In Order To*

A Circle the infinitives of purpose in the following sentences.

Wesley: I'm taking astronomy class in order (to learn) more about the stars and planets.

Zora: I signed up for grammar class to practice my English.

Wesley: I'm taking grammar class in order to strengthen my writing skills. In order to get good grades, we should study together.

Zora: Yes, I would. I like having a study partner to keep me motivated.

Wesley: We should set up a schedule to make sure we study enough.

Zora: I have a day planner to keep me from scheduling two things at once.

Wesley: Let's take a look at it in order to set up our first meeting.

B Read the sentences below. Combine each pair of sentences into one by using an infinitive of purpose.

1. Violet took science class. She wanted to learn more about space.

   Violet took science class in order to learn more about space.

2. The professor wanted to get a closer look at the planets. He used his telescope.

   _____

3. I took out my microscope. I had to observe very small things.

   _____

4. We were hungry for hamburgers. We drove to the restaurant.

   _____

5. You looked out the window. You saw a car pull into the driveway.

   _____

C Write questions using the words in parentheses. Then write answers that are true for you. Make sure to use infinitives in your answer.

1. (you / attend / college)

   Why do you attend college?

   I attend college in order to prepare for a teaching career.

2. (you / study / English)

   _____

   _____

3. (you / go / to class)

   _____

   _____

4. (you / visit / the doctor's office)

   _____

   _____

5. (you / eat / food)

   _____

   _____

Putting It Together

■ GRAMMAR

A Rewrite the sentences that have mistakes. If there are no mistakes, write "C."

1. It's disappointed to get a bad grade.   _It's disappointing to get a bad grade._

2. To see a shooting star is exciting.   _____

3. Is there not too much water on Earth?   _____

4. The professor was excited to grade the papers.   _____

5. It's too cold to wear shorts outside.   _____

6. Your not old enough to drink alcohol.   _____

7. Sean studied in order to pass the test.   _____

8. To prove gravity works he dropped the ball.   _____

9. We took English class improving our grammar.   _____

10. Constantine exercised for lose weight.   _____

B Use adjectives and infinitives to write four sentences about your life.

I was excited to start college last year.

1. _____

2. _____

3. _____

4. _____

C Complete the statements with infinitives. Write sentences that are true for you.

1. I don't have enough time _____ to work out at the gym every day.

2. I'm not old enough _____

3. I'm too tired _____

4. I so happy _____

5. I don't have enough energy _____

■ VOCABULARY

Place each vocabulary word in the grid below.

4 letters	6 letters	8 letters	10 letters
CORE	CRATER	DISCOVER	EXPERIMENT
	LETTER		

5 letters	7 letters	9 letters	11 letters
SPACE	GRAVITY	TELESCOPE	SOLAR SYSTEM
	PLANETS		

Comparatives: -er/More/ Less; Superlatives

PART ONE	Comparatives: -er/More/Less

A Circle the correct form of the comparative to complete each sentence.

1. The comedy show is _____ the drama.

   a. more shorter   (b.) shorter than   c. shortest

2. Uma woke up _____ her roommate.

   a. earlier than   b. earlyer than   c. earlier

3. The car advertisement was done _____ the one for jeans.

   a. less skillfully than   b. less skillfully   c. less skillful than

4. I finished the test _____ the student in the seat next to me.

   a. quickly than   b. more quicker than   c. more quickly than

5. The hallway to media studies is _____ the one to the cafeteria.

   a. more narrow than   b. more narrower than   c. narrow than

6. The first test was _____ the final exam.

   a. simpler than   b. simple than   c. simplest

7. Was the filet _____ the sirloin?

   a. more tenderer than   b. tender than   c. more tender than

8. Norma did _____ Al on the test.

   a. betterer than   b. better than   c. betterer

9. The playing child made _____ the crying baby.

   a. less noise than   b. fewer noise than   c. less noise

10. The library holds _____ the economics classroom.

    a. few people than   b. lesser people than   c. fewer people than

B Complete the sentences below by writing a comparative form of the words in parentheses. Add *more/less/fewer* as needed.

1. Last night's sunset was ___*more beautiful*___ (beautiful) than the previous night's.

2. The basketball player is _____ (tall) than the baseball player.

3. Frederica looked _____ (happy) than Thomas about the test results.

4. The library was _____ (quiet) than the cafeteria.

5. The champion long jumper went _____ (far) than the one who came second.

6. The difficult test worksheet required _____ (time) than the easy one.

7. Gary finished the race _____ (slowly) than Elijah.

8. I have _____ (money) than a lot of other students who get money from their parents.

9. Was the design of the soft drink commercial _____ (simple) than the one for the cell phone?

C Complete each slogan by adding the correct form of a comparative. (Answers will vary.)

1. Our Internet connection is _____ *faster than theirs.* _____

2. Sportco running shoes are _____

3. Westville University is _____

4. Jadaco jewelry is _____

5. Go brand trucks are _____

6. Center Mall is _____

PART TWO   **Superlatives**

A Circle the correct form of the superlative to complete each sentence.

1. Zachary has the _____ grades in the class.

   a. goodest   b. better   c.)best

2. My geology professor is the _____ of all my teachers.

   a. most understanding   b. most understanded   c. understaningest

3. The ballet dancer was the _____ performer in the recital.

   a. most graceful   b. more graceful   c. less graceful

4. This model is the _____ car on the market.

   a. fastest   b. faster   c. most fast

5. That was the _____ test I've ever taken.

   a. most hard   b. least hard   c. hardest

6. Pablo had the _____ mistakes on the exam.

   a. few   b. fewest   c. fewer

7. When we walk up the stairs, Gisella always makes the _____.

   a. less noise   b. least noise   c. noisiest

8. Why do you think that was the _____ movie you've ever seen?

   a. baddest   b. badder   c. worst

B Complete the conversation below using the correct form of the superlatives in the boxes. Each word will be used once. Add *least* or *more* if necessary.

tall	creative	funny	realistic
good	effective	important	successful

Blake: That was the ___least effective___ advertisement for sneakers I've ever seen. It didn't make me want to buy anything.

Luigi: It certainly wasn't the _____ promotional material. It kept showing the same images over and over again.

Blake: I did laugh at the flying chicken.

Luigi: Yes. That was one of the _____ things I've ever seen.

Blake: I always find the _____ ads are memorable.

Luigi: It was memorable, but it wasn't the _____ ad I've ever seen.

Blake: My favorite commercial is a car ad. There are five buildings. The car is driving down the _____ one.

Luigi: I've seen that commercial. It's the _____ car commercial out there. What car can actually drive down a building?

Blake: I still like it. The _____ thing I learned from watching the sneaker ad was to make a commercial memorable. I'm still amused by that flying chicken.

C Write sentences with superlatives using the words in parentheses.

1. (be / good / television show / I / have seen)

   That was the best television show I've ever seen.

2. (the professor / say / my paper / was / creative / in the classroom)

   _____

3. (bright / light / in the dorm room / be / in the bathroom)

   _____

4. (10 miles / be / far / Steve / ever / run)

   _____

5. (my favorite store / have / helpful / salespeople)

   _____

Putting It Together

■ GRAMMAR

A Rewrite the sentences that have mistakes. If there are no mistakes, write "C."

1. The chocolate cake was best than the vanilla cake.

   The chocolate cake was better than the vanilla cake.

2. The commercial said the truck was more fast than the sedan.

   _____

3. Marsha thinks she is prettyer than Helen.

   _____

4. The science major wrote less skillfully than the English major.

   _____

5. Babies born with blue eyes are more commoner than babies born with brown eyes.

   _____

6. I bought less bananas than apples.

_____

7. Their store is very clean, but ours is more clean.

_____

8. That is the less interesting book I've ever read.

_____

9. Harold got the baddest haircut the other day.

_____

10. That new drama was rated the most sad movie of the century.

_____

11. Colombia is the most beautiful country of the world.

_____

12. Celia is the quieter in the classroom.

_____

B **Write comparative sentences using the adjectives or adverbs below. Make comparisons that are true for you.**

1. bad

   My grades in my first semester of college were worse than my second semester grades.

2. early

   _____

3. slowly

   _____

4. quickly

   _____

5. handsome

   _____

6. good

   _____

C **Write questions with superlatives using the words in parentheses. Then write an answer that is true for you.**

1. (good / class / you / take)

   What is the best class you've taken?

   The best class I've taken is astronomy.

2. (interest / person / you / know)

   _____

   _____

3. (low / grade / you / receive)

   _____

   _____

4. (bad / television show / you / watch)

   _____

   _____

5. (surprise / thing / happen / to you)

   _____

   _____

■ VOCABULARY

Unscramble each of the clue words. Copy the letters in the numbered cells to other cells with the same number.

GIRNEKATM TASERGYT ☐☐☐☐☐☐☐☐☐ ☐☐☐☐☐☐☐☐
                    3   9

GOSNAL ☐☐☐☐☐☐
        10 2

MEIRETESDTNAV ☐☐☐☐☐☐☐☐☐☐☐☐☐
                        4

SUONERMC ☐☐☐☐☐☐☐☐
              5

BBLIRODLA ☐☐☐☐☐☐☐☐☐
               6

CUOPSDTR ☐☐☐☐☐☐☐☐
             1

SIDNIECO ☐☐☐☐☐☐☐☐
           7

REEVISC ☐☐☐☐☐☐☐
           8

☐☐☐☐☐☐☐☐☐☐
1 2 3 4 5 6 7 8 9 10

As . . . As for Comparisons; Comparative Expressions: *The Same As/Similar To/ Different From/Like/Alike/Unlike*

PART ONE   **As . . . As for Comparisons**

A Underline the comparative structure in the following sentences. Then identify whether the comparisons are affirmative (+) or negative (-).

1. Her eyes were <u>as blue as</u> the sky.   __+__

2. Luke's feet aren't as long as Ozzy's.   _____

3. Padma laughs as loudly as a hyena.   _____

4. My sister doesn't get in trouble as often as I do.   _____

5. I don't speak as quickly as my best friend.   _____

6. Winonna is as punctual as the tolling of a clock.   _____

7. Lisa doesn't eat as much food as her brother.   _____

8. Mr. Hung doesn't give as many tests as Ms. Taylor.   _____

9. You speak English as well as anyone in the class.   _____

10. I landed as safely as a baby in a crib.   _____

B Complete the sentences by filling in the blanks with a comparative structure. Use the words in the boxes. Each word will be used only once.

patient	dark	free time	beautiful	long
aggressively	lonely	well	question	homework

1. Her hair was _____*as dark as*_____ the night sky.

2. My geology professor didn't assign _____ my physics professor.

3. Philippe ate _____ a lion.

4. Marianne is _____ a sunset.

5. I'm not _____ my mother. She never gets annoyed.

6. Did Blair take the disappointment _____ the others?

7. The first test didn't have _____ the second one.

8. Was Shakespeare's poem _____ Marlowe's?

9. I was _____ a fish without its school.

10. Students who work don't have _____ students who don't work.

C Write similes using the words in parentheses.

1. (her lip / be / red / rose)

_____ Her lips are as red as a rose. _____

2. (Quinn / do not / work / hard / I do)

_____

3. (Daryl / did not perform / skillfully / surgeon)

_____

4. (the athlete / ran / gracefully / gazelle)

_____

5. (I / did not / eat / ice cream / you did)

_____

6. (the salesperson / sell / shoes / the manager)

_____

| PART TWO | **Comparative Expressions:** *The Same As/ Similar To/Different From/Like/Alike/Unlike* |

A Circle the correct choices to complete the sentences.

1. The color of my eyes is _____ the color of my sister's eyes.

   a. similar from   b. similar   c. similar to

2. Movies and television shows are _____.

   a. similar   b. similar to   c. different from

3. Elle's grade was _____ mine.

   a. the same as   b. similar   c. alike

4. A research paper is _____ an exam.

    a. a difference between   b. different from   c. different

5. Is there _____ grammar class and composition class?

    a. a difference between   b. unlike   c. the same as

6. _____ an apartment, a dorm room is smaller than a house.

    a. Similar   b. A difference between   c. Like

7. Dogs are _____ cats.

    a. different   b. unlike   c. similar

8. Poetry and prose are _____.

    a. unlike   b. the same as   c. different

9. _____ poetry, songs have music.

    a. Unlike   b. Are unlike   c. Different from

10. Are the twin brothers _____?

    a. the same as   b. similar to   c. alike

11. The college library is _____ a big classroom.

    a. similar   b. like   c. different

B Complete the sentences by adding a comparative expression. (Answers may vary.)

1. A maple tree is ___*different from*___ an evergreen tree.

2. Is there _____ the two homework assignments?

3. The lyrics of music are _____ poetry.

4. _____ talking, singing requires use of the mouth.

5. Leslie's pantsuit is _____ Tamara's dress.

6. Babies and children are _____ because they both cry often.

7. Trucks and airplanes are _____ because trucks stay on the ground and airplanes don't.

8. _____ walking, sitting doesn't involve a lot of movement.

C Write a sentence that is true for you comparing the two things in parentheses. Be sure to use a comparative expression.

1. (homework assignments / final exams)

     Homework assignments are unlike final exams because exams are harder.

2. (your home country / your current country)

     _____

3. (talking in person / talking on the phone)

     _____

4. (you / your family)

     _____

5. (night / day)

     _____

Putting It Together

■ GRAMMAR

A Rewrite the sentences that have mistakes. If there are no mistakes, write "C."

1. I felt as fresh a spring day.   *I felt as fresh as a spring day.*

2. A carrot is not as sweet as a cupcake.   _____

3. Is Manny act as politely as Pedro?   _____

4. She worked patiently as a saint.   _____

5. That car has as many power as the
   other one.   _____

6. You have as much pairs of shoe as I do.   _____

7. Is snow different to rain?   _____

8. There's a difference from a pen and
   a crayon.   _____

9. Newspapers and magazines are
   similar to.   _____

10. Unlike speaking singing has rhythm.   _____

11. Like motorcycles, cars have engines.   _____

12. Her ring is as same as mine.   _____

B Use the words below to write sentences that are true for you. Use a comparative structure in each sentence.

1. (difficult) _My first semester in college wasn't as difficult as my second semester._

2. (quietly) _____

3. (strong) _____

4. (tall) _____

5. (many classes) _____

6. (much ambition) _____

C Write sentences that are true for you using the comparative expressions in parentheses.

1. (the same as) _My home country isn't the same as the country I live in now._

2. (similar to) _____

3. (are different) _____

4. (a difference between) _____

5. (like) _____

6. (are alike) _____

7. (unlike) _____

8. (different from) _____

■ VOCABULARY

Unscramble each of the clue words. Copy the letters in the numbered cells to other cells with the same number.

LIEMIS

5				7	

REOTPHAM

	10	8	6	2	9	

LISMIAR

1			3			

POTE

4			

		K							
1	2	3	4	5	6	7	8	9	10

I. Sentence Errors: Fragments

A **Read the information below.**

A sentence fragment is an incomplete sentence. For a sentence to be complete, it must have a subject and a finite verb.

Sentence fragment	Problem	Complete sentence
Is relaxing.	no **subject**	**Music** is relaxing.
The benefits of living in a city.	no finite **verb**	The benefits of living in a city **are** *great*.

B **Write "C" if the sentence is complete or "F" if it's a fragment. If it's a fragment, correct it by adding a subject or finite verb.**

1. They were at the mall last Saturday. _____

2. Mayans in Mexico. _____

3. Your favorite teacher in high school. _____

4. On vacation last week. _____

5. There are a lot of shops. _____

6. A Portugese sailor. _____

7. Next to the train station. _____

8. The fish swim. _____

9. One park near the hotel. _____

10. This town has. _____

II. Using Major and Minor Details

C *Major supporting details* in a paragraph are important pieces of information that directly support the main point or topic sentence. *Minor supporting details* are smaller pieces of information that support major details.

D Read the paragraph below. Match the numbers with the items below.

> ❶In my country, young people don't become independent quickly. ❷One reason for this is economic. ❸There aren't a lot of jobs in my country.

Topic Sentence: _____

Major supporting detail: _____

Minor supporting detail: _____

E Read the paragraph. Find the major details and underline them once. Find the minor details and underline them twice.

> In my country, young people don't become independent quickly. One reason for this is economic. There aren't a lot of jobs in my country. Costs are high and salaries are low. Young people can't afford to live alone. Another reason is that families have very close relationships. Parents want their children to live with them as long as possible. When children finally move out of their parent's house, they usually do not move far away.

F Read the paragraph again.

G Answer the questions about the paragraph.

1. What is the topic sentence?

   _____

2. What major details does the writer give to support the topic sentence?

   _____

3. What minor details does the writer give to support the major details?

   _____

4. How does the writer present the major details? What words or phrases are used?

   _____

5. What kind of information directly supports the topic sentence?

   _____

H Choose a topic that interests you from Lessons 11–20 of your student book. Use the chart below to write about the topic.

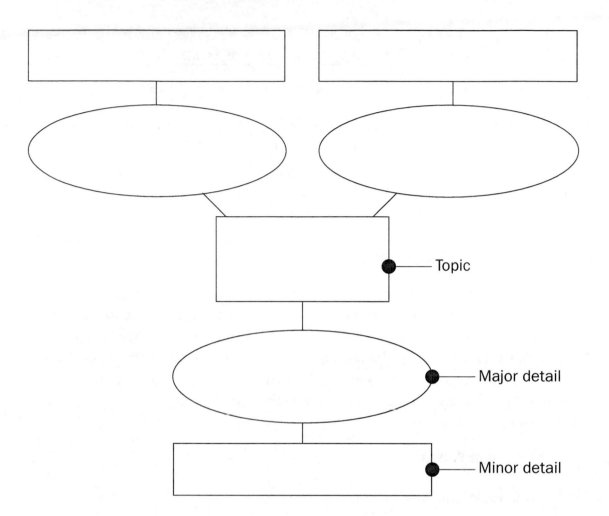

Topic

Major detail

Minor detail

I Write a paragraph about your topic.

J **Check your paragraph. Use the checklist.**

	Yes	No
There are no sentence fragments.		
There is a topic sentence.		
There are major and minor supporting details.		
There is a concluding sentence.		

K **Rewrite your paragraph.**

Advice, Rules, and Obligations: *Should/Ought To/Had Better; Be Supposed To*

A Circle the correct answers to complete the sentences.

1. Journalists _____ articles with the facts.

   a. should to write   (b.) should write   c. had better to write

2. Writers _____ the finer points of grammar.

   a. had better know   b. had better to know   c. had better knows

3. A journalist _____ the reader.

   a. ought to know   b. ought know   c. had ought know

4. Students _____ on tests.

   a. shouldn't cheat   b. shouldn't cheats   c. shouldn't cheated

5. We _____ so many sweets.

   a. ought to not eat   b. ought not eat   c. ought not eats

6. You _____ another journalism class.

   a. had better miss not   b. had not miss   c. had better not miss

7. _____ the journalist _____ the interview here?

   a. Had better / conduct   b. Should / conduct   c. Ought to / conduct

8. _____ newspapers _____ the readers the facts?

   a. Should / tell   b. Should / tells   c. Had better / tell

B Fill in the blanks with the correct form of the word in parentheses. Add *not* when you think it's needed.

1. Everyone (should) _____*should*_____ eat healthy foods.

2. We (had better) _____ eat too much junk food.

3. You (should) _____ shout when the baby is sleeping.

4. Mario (ought to) _____ get his homework done before class starts.

5. The professor (had better) _____ grade the papers before the semester ends.

6. (Should) _____ they follow the rules of the game?

7. The journalist (ought to) _____ write lies in the news story.

8. (Should) _____ Nadia read the directions on the test?

C Fill in the blanks with the correct form of the words in parentheses and by adding *should/had better/ought to*. Add *not* when you think it's needed. (Answers will vary.)

1. The photo of the burning house (run) ___*ought to run*___ next to the story about the fire.

2. I (review) _____ the article before I send it to the editor.

3. We (print) _____ articles that have unreliable sources.

4. The students (study) _____ for the physics test.

5. Bobbie and Cathy (leave) _____ the restaurant without paying the bill.

6. I (eat) _____ another cookie before dinner.

7. (journalist ask) _____ permission to conduct an interview?

8. The campus cafeteria (carry) _____ more healthy choices.

9. The library (stay) _____ open later on weeknights.

10. (we run) _____ in order to train for the cross country season?

PART TWO   *Be Supposed To*

A Indicate whether the sentences below are affirmative (+) or negative (-).

1. I'm supposed to pick up my sister at the mall.   ___+___

2. You were supposed to stop by the grocery store.   _____

3. We're supposed to do the review tomorrow.   _____

4. The students aren't supposed to cheat on tests.   _____

5. Odell isn't supposed to work today. _____

6. Are they supposed to include the story in this issue? _____

7. Valencia and Giordano are supposed to meet in the library. _____

8. He wasn't supposed to drive the car today. _____

9. Is Donna supposed to write the article? _____

10. Was she supposed to study with us? _____

11. You aren't supposed to make up stories for the newspaper. _____

12. Were they supposed to do that yesterday? _____

B **Complete the blanks with the correct form of *be supposed to*. Add *not* and a pronoun if needed.**

1. The information _was supposed to be_ included in the article.

2. The editor _____ leave before reviewing the newspaper.

3. What time _____ at the office?

4. What _____ do with the picture on the table?

5. The professor _____ take us on that field trip.

6. Gaston and Belle _____ go on a date tomorrow.

7. _____ interview the businessman last week?

8. She _____ take the test until Friday.

9. You _____ study with me in the library.

10. We _____ do that last week.

11. When _____ finish the layout of the newspaper?

12. The article _____ ready by the end of the day.

C **Write sentences with the words in parentheses. Add the correct form of *be supposed to*. Add *not* if necessary.**

1. (I / cook / the chicken / on high)

   I wasn't supposed to cook the chicken on high.

2. (you / meet / me / at 5:30)

   _____

3. (Catalina / have / the article / ready / until tomorrow)

_____

4. (the students / take / a quiz / next Wednesday)

_____

5. (the journalist / be rude / to interviewees)

_____

Putting It Together

GRAMMAR

A Rewrite the sentences that have mistakes. If there are no mistakes, write "C."

1. I should to get my mom to visit me at school.   *I should get my mom to visit me at school.*

2. My mom ought know that I miss her.   _____

3. The teacher had better test the students soon.   _____

4. Ought they work so late on a school night?   _____

5. Desiree should'nt wait to write her paper.   _____

6. The editor ought not to make any mistakes.   _____

7. You had better not to get in any more trouble.   _____

8. We weren't to supposed be leaving yet.   _____

9. Wilma are supposed to go to the doctor.   _____

10. Was Jenny supposed to tip the waitress?   _____

11. Is she to supposed have her article written?   _____

B Write sentences using the words in parentheses. Write something that is true for you.

1. (ought to) _____ *I ought to study more often.* _____

2. (should) _____

3. (had better) _____

4. (shouldn't) _____

5. (ought not) _____

6. (had better not) _____

C Use *who/what/when/where/why/how* and the words in parentheses to write questions. Then write answers that are true for you.

1. (should / you / be do / tomorrow)

   What should you be doing tomorrow?

   I should be studying for a test tomorrow.

2. (should / you / be do / next week)

   _____

   _____

3. (should / you / study with)

   _____

   _____

4. (should / you / take / your / next test)

   _____

   _____

5. (should / you / feel / when you graduate)

   _____

   _____

D Write questions using the words in parentheses and the correct form of *be supposed to*. Then write a short answer. Answer statements will vary.

1. (Blanche / write / articles / for each issue / of the newspaper)

   Is Blanche supposed to write articles for each issue of the newspaper?

   Yes, she is.

2. (the professor / meet / with his students / tomorrow)

   _____

   _____

3. (you / review / the newspaper / for grammatical errors)

   _____

   _____

4. (the athletes / have / a game / at the stadium / this afternoon)

   _____

   _____

5. (Jose / work / in the newspaper office / yesterday)

_____

_____

■ VOCABULARY

Complete the clues and solve the puzzle.

Across

3. A meeting where one person asks another person questions.

Down

1. The _____ wrote an article for the local newspaper.

2. Examples of these include newspapers, magazines, and television shows.

4. The _____ was supposed to interview the anthropology professor for the school newspaper.

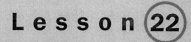
Necessity and Prohibition: Must/Must Not/Have To/Don't Have To; Possibility and Permission: May/Might/ Can/Could/Do You Mind If

PART ONE Necessity and Prohibition: *Must/Must Not/Have To/Don't Have To*

A Circle the letter of the correct answer to complete the sentence.

1. Gerard _____ any mistakes on his tax forms.

   a. must not avoid   (b.) must avoid

2. Wage earners _____ the deadline for filing their taxes.

   a. must not miss   b. must miss

3. I _____ all the required classes in order to graduate.

   a. have to pass   b. don't have to pass

4. My parents _____ me money now that I have a job.

   a. have to give   b. don't have to give

5. _____ attend class everyday?

   a. Do we have to   b. Does we have to

6. _____ complete their taxes yesterday?

   a. Must they   b. Did they have to

7. Zora _____ when she fills out her tax forms.

   a. doesn't have to lie   b. must not lie

8. The students _____ their papers last week.

   a. had to hand in   b. must hand in

B Complete the sentences with *must, must not, have to, don't have to, had to,* or *didn't have to.*

1. Hugo _____ *must* _____ file his taxes by next Thursday.

2. We _____ leave any blank spaces.

3. Leslie _____ take the exam today or she'll fail the class.

4. The professors _____ meet this week. They could meet next week.

5. _____ Courtney pay taxes every year?

6. The cashier _____ charge me taxes on my purchase last night.

7. The students _____ answer all the questions on last night's exam.

C Complete the sentences by filling in the blanks with the correct form of *have to* or *must*. Use the negative form when necessary. Answers may vary.

1. An accountant _____ *must* _____ be able to deal with lots of numbers.

2. I _____ study too hard for my French exam because French is my native language.

3. Does the bank _____ pay me interest on my savings account?

4. You _____ forget to hand in your literature paper.

5. Olga _____ take a physics class because it's part of her major requirements.

6. _____ we pay our taxes by April 15th?

7. Anton _____ take the class again because he passed it the first time.

8. The professor _____ grade the papers by the end of the week.

9. I _____ make too many mistakes on my exam or I'll fail.

10. You _____ put your dog on a leash when you're in the park.

11. I _____ wake up early tomorrow. I want to go running.

12. Everyone who drives _____ get a driver's license.

13. We _____ talk on the phone every night. We see each other every day.

14. You _____ pay me back. It was only $2.00.

| PART TWO | Possibility and Permission: *May/Might/Can/Could/Do You Mind If* |

A Indicate whether the sentences below are about possibility or permission.

1. I might be able to get to class on time.   _____ *possibility* _____

2. Do you mind if I borrow your bike?   _____

3. I might not be able to run a mile. _____

4. Kelly can't file her own paperwork. _____

5. Can you help me with my taxes? _____

6. Could I cancel our appointment? _____

7. You cannot borrow any money. _____

8. Can you answer all the questions or
   are they too difficult? _____

9. May Alexander turn in the paper tomorrow? _____

10. Do you mind if I pay for dinner tonight? _____

11. Could Svetlana use your computer? _____

B Complete the sentences by circling the correct word. Then indicate whether the sentences express possibility or permission.

1. The students (might / can) be in class right now. ___*possibility*___

2. You (might / may) go home if you want to. _____

3. Danielle (can't / might not) have saved any paperwork. _____

4. Eduardo (can't / couldn't) go on the trip. He had to work. _____

5. (Do you mind if / Could) we qualify for a homeowner
   deduction? _____

6. An accountant (may / can) have to review your tax filing. _____

7. A journalist (might not / cannot) make up statistics
   for an article. _____

8. (Can / Do you mind if) you help me study for the
   English exam? _____

9. (Do you mind if / Can't) I use your bathroom? _____

10. (Can / May) she run a ten kilometer race? _____

11. You (may / might) use my computer. _____

12. We (may not / couldn't) speak to the instructor.
    He wasn't in his office. _____

C Use *may/might/can/could/do you mind if* to write questions using the words in parentheses. Then write short answers in response. Answer statements may vary.

1. (we / take / the bus / to the mall)

   May we take the bus to the mall?

   Yes, you may.

2. (Stacie / graduate / without / take / any science classes)

3. (you / deduct / your school expenses / on your taxes)

4. (I / use / the textbook / while take / the test)

5. (the professor / reschedule / class / for tomorrow)

Putting It Together

GRAMMAR

A Rewrite any sentences that have mistakes. If there are no mistakes, write "C."

1. The students must take the test yesterday.

   The students must take the test today.

2. My accountant have to do my taxes.

3. I had to train in order to make the team.

4. She doesn't must pay taxes this year.

5. Sheila must not leave her laptop unattended.

6. Does Anna has to be there by 5:00?

7. Must Hunter pay his taxes?

8. They maybe a little late. _____

9. I cant get an answer from my friend. _____

10. May you file your taxes by yesterday? _____

11. My brother may not borrow my car. _____

12. Do you mind if I set the alarm? _____

B Use *must/have to/must not* to write questions with the words in parentheses. Then write a short answer. Answer statements may vary.

1. (we / hand in / our tax forms / on time)

   _____ Must we hand in our tax forms on time? _____

   _____ Yes, you must. _____

2. (the students / eat / in the school cafeteria)

   _____

   _____

3. (an accountant / file / your taxes)

   _____

   _____

4. (we / speak / during an exam)

   _____

   _____

5. (Beau and Gina / pay / taxes / this year)

   _____

   _____

C Write a question asking for permission for something by using the words in parentheses.

1. (may) _____ May I borrow the car tomorrow? _____

2. (might) _____

3. (do you mind if) _____

4. (can) _____

5. (could) _____

Find the words in the puzzle below and circle them.

```
F  F  C  B  B  I  W  N  I  L  T  I  R  K  H
T  V  O  D  T  P  U  A  C  W  E  M  A  L  X
A  C  B  R  H  G  T  T  A  F  P  A  U  G  X
B  W  Q  V  M  I  H  S  X  V  E  S  E  Q  B
E  T  K  N  P  U  T  B  W  E  W  V  Z  V  A
J  W  E  O  H  P  L  P  L  S  I  L  Y  L  L
X  O  Y  J  I  M  B  A  X  U  L  K  Y  P  R
B  A  I  E  P  G  A  X  K  B  N  H  Z  O  W
Z  A  C  T  L  O  H  D  F  T  I  E  K  C  S
Z  E  L  A  Y  S  S  C  Q  R  U  G  N  J  U
R  Z  K  X  Q  M  P  M  T  A  G  F  J  O  V
O  K  L  E  N  T  D  J  P  C  B  R  N  Z  X
P  V  A  S  E  V  C  S  R  T  A  Y  B  A  L
T  Z  S  K  Y  E  Z  I  U  G  C  S  N  P  P
Z  R  C  M  Q  R  R  N  M  M  H  R  H  H  A
```

FORMULA

RECEIPTS

SUBTRACT

SUM

TAXES

Polite Requests: *Can/Could/Will/Would/Would You Mind?*; Preferences: *Like/Would Like/Prefer/Would Prefer/Would Rather*

PART ONE   Polite Requests: *Can/Could/Will/Would/Would You Mind?*

A Read the situation. Then write a request using *could you, can you, would you mind, would you,* or *will you.* Answers will vary.

1. Your car broke down. You need to get to class. Your friend drives every day.
   Could you please give me a ride to class?

2. Your friend has a book you want to read.
   _____

3. You want to discuss your grades with your instructor.
   _____

4. You need to find a new place to live. Your friend lives in an apartment alone.
   _____

5. You need Thursday off from work. Your coworker doesn't work on Thursdays.
   _____

6. You're giving a friend directions to your house. You want him or her to listen closely.
   _____

7. You're in the cafeteria. You forgot to bring money. Your friend has money.
   _____

8. You're on the phone with a friend. Your mother calls on the other line.
   _____

B Write a question with *can* for <u>possibility</u>. Then complete the short answer.

1. (you / see / the board) _____ *Can you see the board?* _____
   Yes, _____ *I can.* _____

2. (we / open the door) _____

   No, _____

3. (she / drive a motorcycle) _____

   Yes, _____

4. (they / call after 11 PM) _____

   No, _____

5. (I / hand in my work tomorrow) _____

   Yes, _____

C Circle the best answer.

1. Would you mind _____?

   a. let me see your paper   b. let's see your paper   (c.) letting me see your paper

2. Can you _____?

   a. give me another   b. giving me another   c. gave me another
       chance   chance   chance

3. Will you _____?

   a. to wait, please   b. wait, please   c. waiting

4. Would you _____?

   a. stay five more   b. staying five more   c. to stay.
       minutes   minutes

5. _____ showing me your exercise routine?

   a. Can you   b. Could you   c. Would you mind

6. _____ do rigorous exercise?

   a. Will you   b. Can you   c. Would you mind

7. Could you do 200 sit-ups? _____

   a. Yes, I could.   b. No, I wouldn't   c. No, I'm sorry.

PART TWO   **Preferences: *Like/Would Like/Prefer/Would Prefer/Would Rather***

A Complete each sentence with the verb in parentheses.

1. I prefer _to exercise OR exercising_ (exercise) at a gym.

2. I would rather _____ (study) at night than in the morning.

3. I would like _____ (talk) to my instructor about my grades.

4. They'd rather not _____ (work) tonight.

5. My father likes _____ (get up) early in the morning.

6. My family would prefer _____ (take) a vacation together.

7. We like _____ (go) to the gym together.

8. Gerardo prefers_____ (eat) fish.

9. My sister prefers _____ (read).

10. I'd rather not _____ (go) on a diet.

B Write the question for the answer given. (Answers may vary.)

1. _____ *Do you prefer to run outside or run on a treadmill?* _____

I prefer to run outside than run on a treadmill.

2. _____

I would rather join the gym for three months than for one year.

3. _____

I would prefer taking an aerobics class to running three miles.

4. _____

I would like to lift weights.

5. _____

I like walking better than running.

6. _____

I like to take group fitness classes.

7. _____

I would prefer not to join a gym for a year.

8. _____

I would rather not lift weights.

C Circle the best answer.

1. Do you prefer to rent movies or go to the movies?
   a. I'd prefer to rent movies.
   b. I prefer to rent movies.
   c. Both a and b are correct.

2. Would you like to go out to dinner or cook at home?
   a. I'd like to go out to dinner.
   b. I like to go out to dinner.
   d. Both a and b are correct.

3. Would you rather go out on a Friday or on a Saturday?
   a. I rather go out on a Saturday.
   b. I'd rather go out on a Friday.
   c. Both a and b are correct.

4. Would you prefer I call you or you call me?
   a. I'd prefer you to call me.
   b. I'd like you to call me.
   c. Both a and b are correct.

5. Do you like walking to work or driving?
   a. I'd like walking to work.
   b. I like walking to work.
   c. Both a and b are correct.

6. Do you prefer red meat or chicken?
   a. I prefer chicken.
   b. I like chicken.
   c. Both a and b are correct.

7. Would your parents like to sit apart or sit next to each other?
   a. They like sitting next to each other.
   b. They'd like to sit next to each other.
   c. Both a and b are correct.

8. Would you rather pay now or pay later?
   a. I would rather pay now or later.
   b. I'd rather pay now than later.
   c. Both a and b are correct.

Putting It Together

GRAMMAR

A Rewrite the sentences that have mistakes. If there are no mistakes, write "C."

1. I would rather not doing sit-ups.   *I would rather not do sit-ups.*

2. May you help my son with his homework?   _____

3. Would you rather run on a treadmill and run outside?

_____

4. I like playing soccer.

_____

5. Sue likes playing basketball than playing soccer.

_____

6. Will you help me with this project, please?

_____

7. My wife would prefer dieting than exercising.

_____

8. Would you mind helping us move?

_____

9. Will you to lend me your notes?

_____

10. I'd rather to work with a personal trainer.

_____

11. Can you please telling us where to go? _____

12. Could I borrow some money? _____

B Complete the dialogs. Answers will vary.

1. Sam: ___Could you___ study with us tonight?

   Vero: But it's Friday! _____ like to go to the movies or something.

   Sam: But you're the best math student. _____ you please come over and help us?

   Vero: Oh, OK.

2. Ana: Jorge, _____ showing me your English exam?

   Jorge: _____. Didn't you get a good grade?

   Ana: No. _____ please study with me next time?

   Jorge: _____. _____ studying in the library or in the cafeteria?

   Ana: _____ the library. It's less noisy.

3. Juan: Let's put some music on. What kind of music do you like, Linda?

   Linda: _____ rock and some pop. What about you?

   Juan: _____ listen to rock than pop.

   Linda: _____ play that new album by Codex?

   Juan: _____ rather listen to something by Antibalas.

   Linda: Ok. I like them too.

4. Arno: _____ to eat Asian food, tonight?

   Debra: I really like Asian food. But tonight _____ Italian.

   Arno: OK, _____ Italian American or authentic Italian?

   Debra: Authentic. _____ call Casa Mia for a reservation?

   Arno: Sure. _____ eat at 7:00 or 8:00?

   Debra: 8:00.

   Arno: Do you want to go to the movies after?

   Debra: _____ not. I have to get up early.

   Arno: OK.

■ VOCABULARY

Use the clues to solve the puzzle.

Across

4. Feeling strong is a _____ of frequent exercise.

5. _____ is very important after you exercise.

7. My arms and shoulders were sore after only one _____ !

8. I run on a _____ when it's cold or rainy outside.

Down

1. I do this at the gym five days a week.

2. I do this exercise to strengthen my abdomen.

3. I lift these at the gym.

6. Lifting weights builds these.

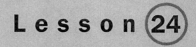

Present Perfect: Statements/Questions/ Short Answers; *Ever/Never/Not Ever*

PART ONE Present Perfect: Statements/Questions/Short Answers

A Complete the sentences with the present perfect of the verbs in parentheses.

1. I _____ *have had* _____ (have) a lot of practical experience in the hospital this semester.

2. We _____ (not work) at all in the hospital this semester.

3. Our professor _____ (give) several lectures on preparing medications.

4. She _____ (teach) us many things.

5. I _____ (help) patients get up and walk around after surgery.

6. The other students _____ (not change) bandages yet.

7. I _____ (bring) some patients their meals.

8. We _____ (see) a lot of movies lately.

9. My friend _____ (take) the test already.

10. They _____ (have) tests all week long.

11. You _____ (take) the wrong coat by accident.

12. My family _____ (be) away for two weeks on vacation.

B Write a question in the present perfect with the words in parentheses. Then complete the short answer.

1. (there / be / any problems / at work) _Have there been any problems at work?_

   No, _____ *there haven't.* _____

2. (you / enjoy / the class) _____

   Yes, _____

3. (you / do / your / homework) _____

    No, _____

4. (your parents / be / to Europe) _____

    Yes, _____

5. (you / work / there / for a long time) _____

    No, _____

6. (she / understand / assignment) _____

    Yes, _____

7. (we / see / that movie) _____

    No, _____

8. (Kevin / give / his paper / to the instructor) _____

    Yes, _____

9. (you / take / anyone's blood pressure) _____

    No, _____

10. (you / hook up / an IV) _____

    Yes, _____

C Write an information question with the words given. Then give a true answer.

1. (How many times / be / to the hospital) *How many times have you been to the hospital?*

    I've been to the hospital once.

2. (Where / go / on vacation) _____

    _____

3. (Where / work / during the past year) _____

    _____

4. (How many / animals / have) _____

    _____

5. (What / do / today) _____

    _____

6. (Where / your parents / live) _____

_____

7. (How many / years / study / English) _____

_____

8. (What / eat / today) _____

_____

<table>
<tr><td>PART TWO</td><td>*Ever/Never/Not Ever*</td></tr>
</table>

A **Write questions in the present perfect with *ever*. Then give a true short answer. If the answer is negative use *never* or *not ever*.**

1. be on TV ___ Have you ever been on TV? Yes, I have. OR No, I never have.

___ OR No, not ever.

2. cheat on an exam _____

_____

3. drive a sports car _____

_____

4. go skiing _____

_____

5. sleep in a tent _____

_____

6. see the ocean _____

_____

7. been in a car accident _____

_____

8. win an award _____

_____

9. laugh until you cried _____

_____

10. receive perfect grades in all your classes _____

_____

B Give a **negative long** answer to the question.

1. Have you ever ridden a horse before?

   I've never ridden a horse.

2. Have you ever run ten miles before?

   _____

3. Have you ever visited Hawaii before?

   _____

4. Have you ever read a novel in English?

   _____

5. Have you ever flown an airplane?

   _____

6. Have you ever gone out with a famous person?

   _____

7. Have you ever bungee jumped?

   _____

Putting It Together

GRAMMAR

A Rewrite the sentences that have mistakes. If there are no mistakes, write "C."

1. She has ever worked in an office.   *she has never worked in an office.*

2. My friend hasn't ever given me bad advice.   _____

3. My mother never has yelled at me.   _____

4. We've not ever argued.   _____

5. You have ever been in a car accident?   _____

6. We haven't bringed lunch.   _____

7. I haven't misunderstood the
   instructions.   _____

8. Has she went to the party?   _____

9. No, she not ever has.   _____

10. I've given a lot a time to this project.   _____

11. Have you never given a shot to anyone?   _____

12. The doctor has written a prescription.   _____

B **Complete the dialog. Use _ever_ or _never_ when necessary.**

Emily: ___*Have you been*___ (be) up all night?

Liza: Yes. I'm really tired.

Emily: Go to bed.

Liza: I can't. I _____ (finish) my paper. It's due tomorrow.

Emily: I _____ (not stay) up all night.

Liza: I _____ (not write) a term paper in a long time. I forgot
how much work it is.

Emily: _____ (ask) your professor for more time?

Liza: No, _____. I _____ (not request) more time
on anything.

Emily: Neither have I.

Liza: Anyway. It's Sunday. It's due tomorrow. My professor
_____ (not give) us her home number.

Emily: Too bad.

Liza: _____ (do) a term paper in two days?

Emily: Yes, _____. I don't think it was very good.

Liza: I don't think mine is very good. But I _____ (read) it yet.

Emily: And you still _____ (finish) it!

Liza: Oh, gosh. I have to get back to work. I'll talk to you later.

Use the clues to solve the puzzle.

Across

5. The doctor prescribed _____.

6. The nurse gave me five _____.

8. The nurse put the _____ on my arm.

9. The nurse read the patient's _____.

10. The nurse gave me a _____.

Down

1. The food was on the _____.

2. The nurse took my _____ three times today.

3. The _____ came quickly.

4. I've never been in a car _____.

7. The nurse had to _____ emergency CPR.

Already/Yet/Just; Since/For

PART ONE	Already/Yet/Just

A Rewrite the questions using the adverb in parentheses.

1. Have you arrived? (just)

   Have you just arrived?

2. Have they called you? (yet)

   _____

3. Have we passed the library? (already)

   _____

4. Have they received their first assignment? (just)

   _____

5. Have you finished your first draft? (already)

   _____

6. Have you gotten any feedback from the professor? (yet)

   _____

B Write a true answer to each question. Use *just* and *already* in your answer.

1. What have you just done?   *I've just finished exercise A.*

2. What have you already done today? _____

3. Where have you just gone?   _____

4. Where have you already gone today? _____

5. Who have you just spoken to?   _____

6. Who have you already spoken to today? _____

C Complete the dialogs with *just*, *already*, and *yet*.

1. Eduardo: Have you spoken to Teresa _____ *yet* _____?

   Lina: No, not _____.

   Eduardo: I've _____ spoken with her and she said she's looking for you.

   Lina: Do you know what she wants?

   Eduardo: She hasn't finished her French project _____. She needs help.

   Lina: I've _____ told her that I don't have time to help her.

2. David: Have you started working on your essay _____?

   Kika: I've _____ started working on it. What about you?

   David: I haven't started _____. But I've _____ finished my term paper for English.

   Kika: Oh, you're so lucky. I haven't begun that _____.

PART TWO	*Since/For*

A Complete the dialogs with the correct form of the verbs in the box and *since* or *for*. Some verbs may be used more than once.

arrive	be	wait	have
charge	speak	study	live

1. Samantha: _____ Have _____ you _____ spoken _____ to Carla?

   Jin: No one _____ to her _____ she left last week.

2. Hilary: _____ your brothers _____ in the United States yet?

   Mario: They _____ here since Friday.

3. Olivia: _____ you _____ a long time?

   Simbad: I _____ here _____ an hour already.

4. Harry: _____ you _____ your dog for a long time?

   Karen: We _____ him _____ 2006.

5. Librarian: You _____ this book out _____ August
   8th. It's overdue.

   Lisa: _____ you _____ me for it?

   Librarian: Yes. You owe four dollars.

6. Maria: _____ you _____ medicine for a long
   time?

   Abha: I _____ it now _____ four years.

7. Pedro: I _____ in the United States _____
   six months already.

   Angel: I _____ here _____ last June.

B Write the questions with the words in parentheses. Then give true answers using
for or *since*.

1. (How long / live / in your house?) _How long have you lived in your house?_

   (for) _I've lived in my house for eight years._

2. (How long / have / your car) _____

   (since) _____

3. (How long / your parents / be together) _____

   (for) _____

4. (How long / know / your best friend) _____

   (since) _____

5. (How long / use / a computer) _____

   (for) _____

C Complete the sentences by matching a phrase in Column A with the correct phrase
in Column B.

Column A	Column B
1. Since Sheila had a baby, _e_	a. I haven't driven my car much.
2. Since I moved to the city, ___	b. they've argued a lot less.
3. Since we started studying together, ___	c. my English has improved.
4. Since my parents divorced, ___	d. I've paid a lot in property taxes.

5. Since I bought my house, ___
6. Since my sister lost her job, ___
7. Since I started exercising, ___

e. she hasn't been able to go out a lot.

f. she's been pretty depressed.

g. I've lost some weight.

Putting It Together

■ GRAMMAR

A Rewrite the sentences that have mistakes. If there are no mistakes, write "C."

1. I've finished my work yet.   *I've finished my work already.*

2. We just returned three years ago.   _____

3. They've written the first draft.   _____

4. Do you just go to the hospital?   _____

5. He's lived here since six months.   _____

6. I've missed you since you been gone.   _____

7. We've thought about you for years.   _____

8. I've been here since 3:00.   _____

9. Since we moved, I've been very busy cleaning. _____

10. They've sold flowers since 1977.   _____

B Complete the dialogs. Use *already, yet, just, since,* or *for.*

1. Ben: Have you finished your composition _____*yet*_____?

    Kyle: No. I've _____ started my outline. What about you?

    Ben: I _____ completed the final draft.

    Kyle: That's great.

2. Audra: How long have you been here?

    Lidia: I've been here _____ a couple of hours.

    Audra: Wow! _____ 2:00?

    Lidia: Yes.

3. Bela: Have you gotten the assignment yet?

   Selena: Yes. I've had it _____ Monday.

   Bela: Have you worked on it _____?

   Selena: I've _____ finished it.

   Bela: Oh, no! I haven't even started.

■ VOCABULARY

Unscramble each of the clue words. Copy the letters in the numbered cells to other cells with the same number.

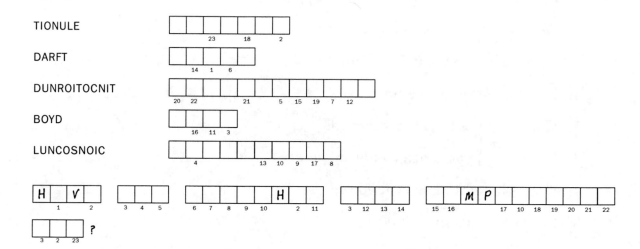

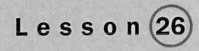

Present Perfect Progressive; Present Perfect vs. Present Perfect Progressive

PART ONE	Present Perfect Progressive

A Write the question with the verbs in parentheses in the present perfect progressive. Then give a true answer.

1. (How long / you / study / English) _How long have you been studying English?_
   I've been studying English for three years.

2. (How long / you / live / in this town) _____

   _____

3. (you / watch TV / a lot / lately) _____

   _____

4. (you / check / your e-mail / in the last hour) _____

   _____

5. (what / you do / for the last hour) _____

   _____

6. (where / you / eat lunch / lately) _____

   _____

B Write the question for the answer.

1. _____ _What have you been watching on TV lately?_ _____

   I've been watching a lot of reality shows on TV lately.

2. _____

   My son's been taking guitar lessons for three years.

3. _____

   We've been talking on the phone for an hour.

4. _____

They've been planning their wedding for a year.

5. _____

We've been taking vacations in Vermont since 2000.

6. _____

I've been thinking about getting another part time job.

A Indicate whether the two sentences have the same (S) meaning or different (D) meanings.

1. a. I've thought about this for two hours.   *S*
    b. I've been thinking about this for two hours.

2. a. I've exercised here since 1999.   _____
    b. I've been exercising here since 1999.

3. a. I've been to five stores.   _____
    b. I've been going to stores.

4. a. We've heard the bell.   _____
    b. We've been hearing the bell.

5. a. She's seen the butterflies.   _____
    b. She's been seeing the butterflies.

6. a. She hasn't felt well.   _____
    b. She hasn't been feeling well.

7. a. The janitor has swept the floors.   _____
    b. The janitor has been sweeping the floors.

8. a. I've written a book.   _____
    b. I've been writing a book.

B Complete the sentences with the present perfect or the present perfect progressive. Then indicate whether the action is completed or continuing.

1. I _have been listening_ (listen) to the radio all day.   *continuing*

2. The teacher _____ (close) the door already. _____

3. We _____ (talk) about going to Florida for _____
the last hour, but we still haven't decided.

4. Who _____ (see) recently? _____

5. _____ (find) your ring? _____

6. I _____ (finish) my term paper. _____

7. I _____ (work) on my term paper,
but I _____ (finish) it yet. _____

8. _____ (spend) a lot of time with _____
your family on weekends?

9. She _____ (climb) Everest several times. _____

10. I _____ (read) the newspaper every day _____
for 40 years.

Putting It Together

■ GRAMMAR

A Rewrite the sentences that have mistakes. If there are no mistakes, write "C."

1. I've answered e-mail all day today.   _I've been answering e-mail_
   all day today.

2. What have you doing? _____

3. I've tried to call them all day long. _____

4. We've already been finishing the puzzle. _____

5. She's been calling three times. _____

6. They've waited at the bus stop for hours. _____

7. I've been thinking about you all day. _____

8. We used e-mail since 1993. _____

9. I've been looking at three magazines. _____

10. The kids have been watching lots of TV. _____

B **Complete the dialogs with the present perfect or the present perfect progressive.**

1. Zara: _____Have you heard_____ (hear) the news? It's all over the media.

    Nico: No. I _____ (not listen) to the radio or watching TV at all today.

    Zara: The Mayor of our town _____ (be) arrested.

    Nico: Wow! What did he do?

    Zara: They're saying that he _____ (steal) money from the town for years.

2. Holly: What _____ (do) lately?

    Rico: I _____ (catch up) on a lot of reading.

    Holly: That's what I want to do! I _____ (able to read) a novel in a long time.

    Rico: I _____ (read) two books this week.

■ **VOCABULARY**

Unscramble each of the clue words. Copy the letters in the numbered cells to other cells with the same number.

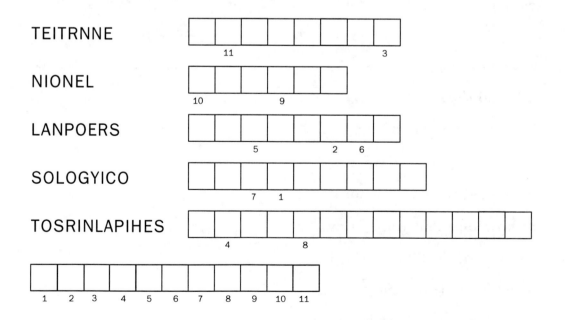

TEITRNNE

NIONEL

LANPOERS

SOLOGYICO

TOSRINLAPIHES

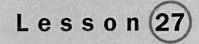

Passive Voice: Forms and Tenses; Passive Voice with the Agent

| PART ONE | Passive Voice: Forms and Tenses |

A Change the sentences from the active voice to the passive voice.

1. They called the doctor to the emergency room.

   The doctor was called to the emergency room.

2. Someone checked the patient's blood pressure.

   _____

3. They made a reservation at a hotel.

   _____

4. They have scheduled several meetings.

   _____

5. We need more bandages.

   _____

6. They rescued a man on the mountain.

   _____

7. They can help the patient.

   _____

8. We take the dog out all the time.

   _____

9. Someone is helping the woman cross the street.

   _____

10. Someone will clean the table off.

    _____

B Read Mary's to do list. Then write about what got done.

To Do	
7:00 AM	Let the dog out.
7:15 AM	Make coffee.
8:00 AM	Wake the kids up.
8:30 AM	Give the kids breakfast.
8:45 AM	Drive the kids to school.
9:30 AM	Do the laundry.
10:00 AM	Water the plants.
10:30 AM	Pay the bills.
11:30 AM	Buy groceries.
12:00 AM	Make lunch.

1. _____ At 7:00 AM the dog was let out. _____

2. _____

3. _____

4. _____

5. _____

6. _____

7. _____

8. _____

9. _____

10. _____

C Write the nurse's responses in the passive.

Doctor: Have you checked the patient's blood pressure?

Nurse: _____ The patient's blood pressure has been checked. _____

Doctor: Did you take her temperature?

Nurse: _____

Doctor: Have you hooked up an IV?

Nurse: _____

Doctor: Did you give her an injection?

Nurse: _____

Doctor: Did someone call her husband?

Nurse: _____

Doctor: Are you observing her closely for changes?

Nurse: _____

Doctor: Are you noting down any changes?

Nurse: _____

Doctor: Have you spoken to admissions?

Nurse: _____

PART TWO	Passive Voice with the Agent

A **Answer the question with an agent.**

1. Who is teaching Spanish 101? (a new teacher)

   Spanish 101 is being taught by a new teacher.

2. Who takes out the garbage every night? (my dad)

   _____

3. How many people have written the new handbook? (five)

   _____

4. How many people visit your Web site every day? (hundreds)

   _____

5. Who is reminding patients about appointments? (the doctor's receptionist)

   _____

6. Who takes care of the horses over the weekend? (local high school girls)

   _____

B **Cross out the agent when it isn't needed.**

1. More traffic lights are needed ~~by everyone~~ in our town.

2. The paper was written by a doctor at our hospital.

3. The child was hit by a drunk driver.

4. ESL classes are offered at the college by college officials.

5. The photocopier was turned on in the morning by someone.

6. Old and sick trees on our street will need to be cut down by workers.

7. The nurse entered and the patient's blood pressure was taken by her.

8. The exams were written by teachers at our school.

9. The midterm exams were taken in November by students.

10. Medical attention is needed by all after a serious accident.

Putting It Together

GRAMMAR

Correct the mistakes. You may have to add or delete words.

A terrible accident ~~was~~ happened in front of my house yesterday. A lot of people were hurted. A car go through a stop sign and then was hit to a truck. At that time, the road was being repair for a construction crew. One of the workers were hit by the car. Another worker was hit by the truck. Both workers took to the hospital by helicopter. The people in the car treated at the scene by paramedics. The truck driver was not injured, but he was very upset. He being questioned by the police. I also questioned the police. It was a terrible day.

Find the words in the puzzle below and circle them.

```
H  Y  A  R  X  G  C  U  E  B  S  A  G  H  I
J  U  F  O  C  V  P  O  H  C  X  L  V  B  V
A  F  X  T  T  E  D  D  I  G  Q  P  S  T  W
U  H  I  A  H  A  H  D  M  L  W  X  F  R  X
X  R  Q  L  S  K  E  S  F  F  Q  I  U  A  H
D  W  H  L  W  M  M  R  I  O  O  D  O  U  I
S  N  I  I  A  G  T  M  X  K  O  Q  H  M  R
T  I  S  R  C  P  U  Y  O  F  P  P  O  A  L
K  W  A  B  U  S  G  R  Y  H  N  R  Q  S  A
G  P  A  I  P  E  Q  W  N  C  W  L  W  D  Y
Y  H  I  F  N  D  D  S  F  E  D  S  Q  T  W
Q  S  G  E  Q  X  O  B  I  M  Y  T  V  F  S
Z  V  L  D  Q  M  P  L  Z  V  W  A  Z  R  T
C  U  H  Z  L  X  S  R  U  Y  P  E  D  T  D
E  Q  U  I  P  M  E  N  T  F  I  L  H  H  Z
```

DEFIBRILLATOR

EQUIPMENT

GURNEY

OXYGEN

PARAMEDICS

TRAUMA

PART ONE	Direct Quotation

A Punctuate the following sentences with quotation marks.

1. "I feel so tired," said Alice as she lay down.

2. He's very handsome she thought.

3. You could go James replied and so could your sister.

4. He insisted Please, please come with us.

5. I wouldn't want to intrude Lily thought to herself.

6. My teacher tells the class every day You should speak to each other in English.

7. That's such a funny joke she laughed.

8. I want to go with you. I don't want to be left behind by myself she whined.

B Punctuate the sentences and add a pronoun and an identifying verb from the box below. Answers may vary slightly.

say	laugh	reply	think	suggest
answer	yell	argue	whisper	insist

1. "I would love a job in the medical field," _____ *he said.* _____

2. Why don't you think about becoming a nurse? _____

3. You're so funny! _____

4. Shhh. Be quiet. The baby's sleeping. _____

5. Please come. It will be fun. _____

6. I don't agree with you at all. _____

7. I would love to come. _____

8. The capital of Argentina is Buenos Aires. _____

9. This is a really beautiful house. I hope they'll accept my offer. _____

10. Come back here! _____

PART TWO   **Reported Statements**

Rewrite the quotes as reported statements. Answers may vary.

1. "Your homework is due tomorrow," the teacher said.

_____ *The teacher said that our homework was due tomorrow.* _____

2. Every weekend our mother always says, "Don't stay out late."

_____

3. "You may use the Internet, as well as books, for your research," the professor said.

_____

4. "We'll meet at the post office and then we'll walk downtown together," said Marcy.

_____

5. "You can take my car," offered Sara.

_____

6. "I'm hoping that this novel will be good," my sister said.

_____

7. "Can I use the phone?" she asked me.

_____

8. "I haven't had pizza in months," he told me.

_____

9. "You should take up swimming. It's great exercise," said my father.

_____

10. "I've been waiting here for hours," said the elderly woman.

_____

11. "You should be here no later than 10:00 AM," he told me.

_____

12. "You need to turn on the TV and watch the news now," my mother advised.

_____

13. "First write an outline and then start a first draft," the teacher told us.

_____

14. "I grew up in a very small village in Alaska," my grandmother said.

_____

Putting It Together

■ GRAMMAR

Circle the correct verb.

Fred: Have you been to class today?

Nona: No, why?

Fred: The instructor (is talking / *was talking*) about the mid-term, the term paper, and the final exam.

Nona: Oh, no. What did she (say / tell)?

Fred: She (said / told) that the mid-term (will / would) be on November 15th.

Nona: Did she say what (will / would) be on the test?

Fred: No. She didn't talk about that. The professor (said / told) that the term paper (will / would) be due on the 17th. She (explains / explained) that we (can / could) use just the Internet to do research if we wanted to.

Nona: That's great.

Fred: Also, she (said / told) that we (can / could) take the final exam home and do it as a take-home test.

Nona: What? Exactly what did she say?

Fred: She said, quote, "You guys may take the test in class or do a take-home test."

Nona: Oh, man! She (said / told) us we (can / could) take it home? That's incredible.

Fred: Not so fast. She also said that the take-home test (will / would) be longer and (may / might) be more difficult.

Nona: Oh, well. I think I still would do the take-home test.

Fred: The professor (said / told) us she was hoping we (will / would) all be there for the next class because she (is going / was going) to give a review.

Nona: I'll be there!

■ VOCABULARY

Use the clues to solve the puzzle.

Across

3. an opinion not based in fact

5. to examine closely

6. direct speech

Down

1. a fictional book

2. to have a high opinion of yourself

4. a person in a novel

Yes/No Reported Questions: Present; *Wh-* Reported Questions: Present

PART ONE   Yes/No Reported Questions: Present

A Rewrite the question as a reported question using the words in parentheses.

1. Do you have any tea?

   (I / if) _____ *I want to know if you have any tea.* _____

2. Are they going to the party?

   (we / whether) _____

3. Does she see a psychologist?

   (the doctor / whether or not) _____

4. Are you interested in joining the team?

   (the coach / whether or not) _____

5. Do we want a review?

   (the teacher / if) _____

6. Do you want to share an apartment?

   (I / whether) _____

7. Do you like to play any sports?

   (my friends / whether or not) _____

8. Are your parents separated?

   (my mother / if) _____

9. Are you a Native American?

   (I / whether) _____

10. Do you know the answer?

    (the teacher / whether) _____

B Write true reported statements about things you would like to know using *if,*
whether, or *whether or not.*

1. _____ I would like to know whether or not it is going to rain tomorrow. _____

2. _____

3. _____

4. _____

5. _____

PART TWO	*Wh-* Reported Questions: Present

A Rewrite the quotes as reported statements using the words in parentheses.

1. Why do we always come home so late?

   (My parents / ask) _My parents are asking why we always come home so late._

2. Why do we need to get permission to quote someone in an interview?

   (the professor / want to know) _____

3. Who do we need to talk to about changing a grade?

   (I / want to know) _____

4. What do we have to review before the test on Friday?

   (we / would like to know) _____

5. Who wrote that song?

   (my teacher / want to know) _____

6. Why do students get nervous during tests?

   (we / want to find out) _____

7. How old is your son?

   (they / ask) _____

8. What course do you want to register for?

   (the administrator / want to know) _____

9. How many languages do you speak?

   (the instructor / ask) _____

10. Where do students go to register for classes?

   (I / want to know) _____

B Write true reported statements about things you would like to know using *wh*-words.

   1. _____ *I want to know how the stock market works.* _____

   2. _____

   3. _____

   4. _____

   5. _____

Putting It Together

GRAMMAR

Rewrite the sentences that have mistakes. If there are no mistakes, write "C."

   1. I want to know are you happy?

   _____ *I want to know if you are happy.* _____

   2. Scientists want to know theories are correct.

   _____

   3. The police are asking where do we live?

   _____

   4. My parents want to know whether or not I'm going to go to college.

   _____

   5. I'd like to know who teaches that class?

   _____

   6. Psychologists want to know what causes depression.

   _____

   7. The application asks how old are we.

   _____

8. My parents would like to know which school I want to attend.

_____

9. The survey is asking where do we live.

_____

10. I want to know are we going to go tonight?

_____

11. The counselor wants to know how you do feel during an exam.

_____

12. The operator asks what telephone extension you need.

_____

■ VOCABULARY

Complete the clues to solve the puzzle.

Across

2. We helped the researcher gather
   _____ for his study.

5. I recently participated in a
   _____ on sleeping habits.

Down

1. She got in trouble for her
   poor _____.

3. Juan was very _____
   about his final exam.

4. The study of human emotion
   and behavior is _____.

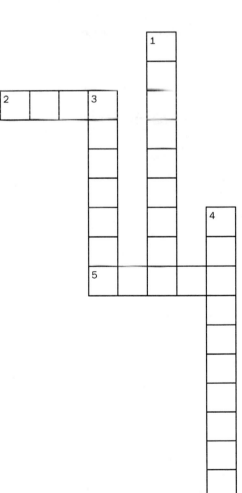

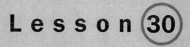

Past Review: Simple Past, Past Progressive, *Used To/Would*; Present Review: Simple Present, Present Progressive, Present Perfect, Present Perfect Progressive; Future Review: Simple Future, Future Progressive

PART ONE	Past Review: Simple Past, Past Progressive, *Used To/Would*

A **Circle the letter of the best answer.**

1. I _____ a new fax machine last night.

   a. did buy   b. bought   c. buyed

2. When my father _____ my age, he _____ a computer.

   a. was / didn't used   b. was / didn't used to   c. was / didn't use

3. After the accident _____, I _____ a text message to my parents.

   a. happened / send   b. was happening / sent   c. happened / sent

4. When the lights _____ out, my mother _____ a shower.

   a. went / was taking   b. were going / was taking   c. went / took

5. We _____ to public school, but now we go to private school.

   a. use to go   b. used to go   c. would go

6. My instructor _____ me a good grade on my composition.

   a. gived   b. did give   c. gave

7. In the 1940s families _____ to the radio together in the evenings.

   a. would listen   b. were listening   c. could listen

8. Last night I _____ to the radio all evening.

   a. would listen   b. was listening   c. could listen

9. The player _____ the ball and then _____ it.

   a. caught / droped   b. catched / droped   c. caught / dropped

10. I _____ computers were difficult. Now I love using them.

    a. use to think   b. used to think   c. would think

11. While we _____, the door _____.

    a. were talking /   b. talked / was slamming   c. were talking / close
       slammed

12. I _____ like chocolate, but now I love it.

    a. didn't use to   b. didn't used to   c. not used to

B Write the questions using the words in parentheses and *used to*. Then complete the short answer.

1. (you / write / with / a typewriter) _Did you use to write with a typewriter?_
                                          Yes, I did.

2. (your class / meet / in the library) _____
   No, _____

3. (Ivan / live / in New York) _____
   Yes, _____

4. (you / go / to school / by bus) _____
   No, _____

5. (your brother / be married) _____
   Yes, _____

C Write the questions using the words in parentheses and *used to*. Then give a true answer.

1. (what / you / call your mother) _What did you use to call your mother?_
                             We used to call her Mommy.

2. (where / go / to college) _____
   _____

3. (Where / you / live) _____
   _____

4. (what / you / eat / in your home country) _____
   _____

5. (what / TV programs / watch / when you were younger)? _____

_____

A **Circle the letter of the best answer.**

1. I _____ the Internet since 1994.

   a. use   (b.) have been using   c. am using

2. The instructor _____ exams on Fridays.

   a. is handing back   b. hands back   c. isn't hand back

3. We _____ to Phoenix now.

   a. are flying   b. have flown   c. fly

4. My sister _____ about going to medical school for years now.

   a. thinks   b. has been thinking   c. is thinking

5. Sometimes we _____ to the park for lunch.

   a. go   b. are going   c. have gone

6. The phone _____ for an hour now.

   a. is ringing   b. rings   c. has been ringing

7. My children always _____ text messages.

   a. sending   b. are sending   c. send

8. We _____ across the Golden Gate Bridge two times.

   a. are walking   b. have walked   c. walk

9. They _____ for five years.

   a. have married   b. have been married   c. are married

10. I _____ more letters lately.

   a. have been writing   b. have written   c. write

B Match a question in Column A with an answer in Column B.

Column A

Column B

1. What have you done to your computer? _c_

a. We've been working out a lot.

2. Where do you like to go to eat? ____

b. I like Texas.

3. Who do you talk to when you have problems? ____

c. I've installed a Webcam.

d. Yes, I am.

4. What does Mr. Zamora do? ____

5. Do you like to use new technology? ____

e. I've been going on Mondays and Fridays.

6. Are you reading a new novel? ____

f. I usually talk to my sister.

7. When have you been going to the gym? ____

g. He's talking on the phone.

8. Where would you like to live, Texas or Iowa? ____

h. Yes, I do.

9. How long have you been in San Francisco? ____

i. I'd like to live in Texas.

10. What have you been doing lately? ____

j. He's a computer technician.

11. What is your brother doing now? ____

k. We've been here since March 21.

12. Which state do you prefer, Texas or Iowa? ____

l. We like to go to a local café.

PART THREE   **Future Review: Simple Future, Future Progressive**

A Write sentences with *will* and the words in parentheses.

1. (he / go / to the mall / tonight)   _He'll go to the mall tonight._

2. (I / help / you / move / on Sunday)   _____

3. (I / promise / I / not / miss / your show)   _____

4. (we / have / a great time)   _____

5. (she / probably / go / to college / in Boston)   _____

6. (you / love / this house)   _____

B Write sentences with *will* and the words in parentheses.

1. (get married) In one year, we _'ll be getting married._

2. (attend) In 20 years, many children _____ virtual schools.

3. (experience) In ten years, we _____ stranger weather.

4. (head) By next week, I _____ to the Bahamas for vacation.

5. (climb) In two years, our manager _____ to the top of the corporate ladder.

6. (retire) In 25 years, I'll _____.

7. (go) My children _____ to school in a few years.

8. (work) I _____ a lot during the next decade.

Putting It Together

■ GRAMMAR

Choose the correct verb or phrase.

Lucia: Hi, Adam. How are you? I (didn't see / haven't seen) you in a long time.

Adam: I know! I'm fine. I (am thinking / have been thinking) about you, actually.

Lucia: Why have you been thinking about me?

Adam: I remember last year (you researched / were researching) graduate schools.

Lucia: (Do you look / Are you looking) at graduate schools now?

Adam: Yes, I am. I (wonder / have been wondering) what I'm going to do next year.

Lucia: (There are not / There are no) a lot of jobs right now.

Adam: I know! There's (anything / nothing).

Lucia: Where do you think you (are applying / will be applying)?

Adam: That's what I've been thinking about. Where (did you apply / you applied)?

Lucia: I (applied / was applying) to State University and to Westville College. Luckily I (did get / got) into both.

Adam: (Did you decide / Were you deciding) on State University or Westville?

Lucia: I (decided / am decided) on State. I (will be starting / start) this September.

Adam: Tomorrow I (will be getting / have gotten) more information on the colleges I'm interested in.

Lucia: Well, good luck! Let me know if you need any help.

Adam: Thanks. I (am going to / will give you a call), I promise!

Find the words in the puzzle and circle them.

```
H  E  K  N  H  A  M  D  Q  G  R  L  H  E  T
A  F  G  X  I  L  N  W  L  W  U  H  Y  N  Y
U  P  L  A  L  Q  L  T  Z  A  S  B  X  I  W
J  M  I  M  S  M  S  H  E  H  V  Z  Y  H  E
R  T  C  D  V  S  I  N  P  N  W  I  C  B
T  S  Z  A  R  E  E  A  G  K  N  D  A  A  C
I  M  C  V  V  R  R  M  Z  C  K  A  V  M  A
S  S  E  R  P  G  N  I  T  N  I  R  P  X  M
Z  U  Q  J  E  P  X  W  X  X  G  I  K  A  J
B  Q  Q  L  H  M  K  R  O  R  E  E  O  F  O
C  X  E  O  N  J  X  H  I  F  N  T  A  U  M
K  T  N  V  I  C  V  X  I  T  C  J  C  A  Y
G  E  N  T  B  K  W  U  D  W  Q  A  W  O  B
M  M  Z  C  O  M  P  U  T  E  R  K  W  F  I
X  E  J  W  O  S  J  K  S  G  C  G  F  P  Q
```

ANTENNA

COMPUTER

FAX MACHINE

PHONE

PRINTING PRESS

TELEGRAPH

TEXT MESSAGE

WEBCAM

I. Formatting a Cover Letter

A Read the business letter. Then label each part of the letter using the words from the box.

the return address	the date	the signature
the inside address	the greeting	the closing

❶ 330 Norton Street
Indianapolis, IN 46201
Tel. 386-555-2922
ve@westville.edu

❷ January 16, 2007

❸ Ms. Carrie Sanders
Universal Hotel
1000 Hotel Plaza
Indianapolis, IN 46201

❹ Dear Ms. Sanders,

I am writing to apply for the summer internship at with Universal Hotel as advertised on your website.

As you can see from my resume, my previous work experience and my status as a Westville University student in my junior year studying business management, make me an excellent candidate for the internship. My experience in sales and customer relations, combined with my courses in business and marketing, have convinced me that hospitality marketing is a career option I would like to explore.

I would enjoy the opportunity to meet with you to discuss the position and my qualifications. I will contact you within a week to arrange a meeting. Should you have any questions before that time, you may reach me via phone (386-555-2922) or via e-mail (ve@westville.edu).

❺ Sincerely,

❻ *Veronica Egas*
Veronica Egas

II. Writing a Cover Letter

B A cover letter is a business letter that usually accompanies a resume in a job application. The cover letter should:

1. explain why you're sending your resume.

2. say how you got the information about the job opening.

3. entice the reader to look at your resume.

4. highlight relevant information about your experience and education.

5. indicate how you plan to follow up.

C Read the cover letter in A again. Write a sentence or phrase from the letter that matches the information a cover letter should have.

1.	*candidate for a summer internship*
2.	
3.	
4.	
5.	

D Find an ad for a job you would like to apply for. Paste or copy the ad in the box below.

E Write a cover letter responding to the ad you found.

[blank lined writing space]

F Exchange cover letters with a classmate. Check your classmate's cover letter.

	Yes	No
It has a standard business letter format.		
It explains why you're sending you resume.		
It explains how you got the information about the job opening.		
It highlights relevant information about your experience and education.		
It indicates how you plan to follow up.		
It states whether your resume is attached.		

G Rewrite your cover letter.

[blank lined writing space]

Grammar Connection Series

Grammar Connection 1
Text 978-1-4130-0830-2
International Student Edition Text 978-1-4130-1750-2
Workbook 978-1-4130-0834-0
Audio CDs 978-1-4130-0831-9
Audio Tapes 978-1-4130-0832-6
Teacher's Annotated Edition (with Activity Bank and Classroom
   Presentation Tool CD-ROM) 978-1-4240-0214-6
Assessment CD-ROM with *ExamView*® 978-1-4130-0850-0

Grammar Connection 2
Text 978-1-4130-0835-7
International Student Edition Text 978-1-4130-1752-6
Workbook 978-1-4130-0839-5
Audio CDs 978-1-4130-0836-4
Audio Tapes 978-1-4130-0837-1
Teacher's Annotated Edition (with Activity Bank and Classroom
   Presentation Tool CD-ROM) 978-1-4240-0216-0
Assessment CD-ROM with *ExamView*® 978-1-4240-0408-9

Grammar Connection 3
Text 978-1-4130-0840-1
International Student Edition Text 978-1-4130-1754-0
Workbook 978-1-4130-0844-9
Audio CDs 978-1-4130-0841-8
Audio Tapes 978-1-4130-0842-5
Teacher's Annotated Edition (with Activity Bank and Classroom
   Presentation Tool CD-ROM) 978-1-4240-0219-1
Assessment CD-ROM with *ExamView*® 978-1-4240-0409-6

Grammar Connection 4
Text 978-1-4130-0845-6
International Student Edition Text 978-1-4130-1756-4
Workbook 978-1-4130-0849-4
Audio CDs 978-1-4130-0846-3
Audio Tapes 978-1-4130-0847-0
Teacher's Annotated Edition (with Activity Bank and Classroom
   Presentation Tool CD-ROM) 978-1-4240-0221-4
Assessment CD-ROM with *ExamView*® 978-1-4240-0410-2

Grammar Connection 5
Text 978-1-4240-0034-0
International Student Edition Text 978-1-4240-0037-1
Workbook 978-1-4240-0041-8
Audio CDs 978-1-4240-0038-8
Audio Tapes 978-1-4240-0039-5
Teacher's Annotated Edition (with Activity Bank and Classroom
   Presentation Tool CD-ROM) 978-1-4240-0222-1
Assessment CD-ROM with *ExamView*® 978-1-4240-0411-9

ELT International Contact Information

United States
Heinle, Cengage Learning
20 Channel Center Street
Boston, MA 02210
U.S.A.
Tel: 617-289-7700
Fax: 617-289-7844

Australia/New Zealand
Tel: 61-(0)3-9685-4111
Fax: 61-(0)3-9685-4199

Brazil
Tel: (55 11) 36659931
Fax: (55 11) 36659901

Canada
Tel: 416-752-9448
Fax: 416-750-8102

China
Tel: 86-10-8286-2095
Fax: 86-10-8286-2089
tlsg.infochina@cengage.com

Japan
Tel: 81-3-3511-4390
Fax: 81-3-3511-4391

Korea
Tel: 82-2-322-4926
Fax: 82-2-322-4927

Latin America
Tel: (52 55) 1500-6000
Fax: (52 55) 1500-6019
Toll Free: 01-800-800-3768

Singapore – Regional Headquarters
Tel: 65-6410-1200
Fax: 65-6410-1208

Taiwan
Tel: 886-2-2558-0569
Fax: 886-2-2558-0360

UK/Europe/Middle East/Africa
Tel: 44-20-7067-2667
Fax: 44-20-7067-2600
elt.info@cengage.com

CPSIA information can be obtained
at www.ICGtesting.com
Printed in the USA
FFOW01n1332150815
16043FF